Praise for *Uses of Literature*

"For decades now, the picture of how we read held by literary theorists and that held by everyday common readers have been galaxies apart. But in this lucid, readable, and highly persuasive book, Rita Felski demonstrates the impossible: that recent literary theorists and common readers not only have something to say to each other, but actually need one another."

*Gerald Graff, Professor of English and Education and 2008 President,*
*Modern Language Association*

"With literature and reading losing their appeal to young people by the year, this manifesto is all the more worthy and timely . . . People are moved by a novel, play, poem. That's what keeps literature alive and makes it important. Why does it happen? *Uses of Literature* explains it, restoring notions discredited in literary study but central to the experience of reading . . . Such a return to basics is just what our fading disciplines need if liberal education is to thrive."

*Mark Bauerlein, Emory University*

"As I would expect from a scholar of this calibre, the quality of thought is very high. What came as an unexpected pleasure was the quality of the writing – which is to say, the directness and clarity, the elegance and wit . . . I am convinced of the value of her [book] as a whole – that is, to 'build better bridges' between literary theory and common knowledge. I thoroughly enjoyed it."

*Gail McDonald, University of Southampton*

"*Uses of Literature* is a lively, sophisticated polemic about literary criticism and literary theorists . . . Extraordinarily well-written, intellectually expansive, [drawing] on a wide range of canonical and popular literature and film to illustrate Felski's compelling account of literary value. And as a teacher, I found her individual chapters to be brimming with possibilities for the classroom, focusing, as they do, on the important heterogeneity of reading experiences."

*Janet Lyon, Pennsylvania State University*

## Blackwell Manifestos

In this new series major critics make timely interventions to address important concepts and subjects, including topics as diverse as, for example: Culture, Race, Religion, History, Society, Geography, Literature, Literary Theory, Shakespeare, Cinema, and Modernism. Written accessibly and with verve and spirit, these books follow no uniform prescription but set out to engage and challenge the broadest range of readers, from undergraduates to postgraduates, university teachers and general readers – all those, in short, interested in ongoing debates and controversies in the humanities and social sciences.

### Already Published

### Forthcoming

Ben —
Manks so much for
your careful
reading + great
suggestions!
Rita

# Uses of Literature

## Rita Felski

**Blackwell**
Publishing

BLACKWELL PUBLISHING
350 Main Street, Malden, MA 02148–5020, USA
9600 Garsington Road, Oxford OX4 2DQ, UK

The right of Rita Felski to be identified as the author of this work has been asserted
in accordance with the UK Copyright, Designs, and Patents Act 1988.

First published 2008 by Blackwell Publishing Ltd

1    2008

*Library of Congress Cataloging-in-Publication Data*

Felski, Rita, 1956–
  Uses of literature / Rita Felski.
    p. cm. — (Blackwell manifestos)
  Includes bibliographical references and index.
  ISBN 978-1-4051-4723-1 (hardcover : alk. paper) — ISBN 978-1-4051-4724-8
(pbk. : alk. paper)    1. Literature—Philosophy.    2. Books and reading.    I. Title.

  PN49.F453 2008
  801—dc22

                                                              2007043479

A catalogue record for this title is available from the British Library.

Set in 11.5/13.5pt Bembo
by Graphicraft Limited, Hong Kong
Printed and bound in Singapore
by Utopia Press Pte Ltd

The publisher's policy is to use permanent paper from mills that operate a sustainable forestry
policy, and which has been manufactured from pulp processed using acid-free and elementary
chlorine-free practices. Furthermore, the publisher ensures that the text paper and cover
board used have met acceptable environmental accreditation standards.

For further information on
Blackwell Publishing, visit our website at
www.blackwellpublishing.com

# Contents

# Acknowledgments

My thanks go first of all to Emma Bennett at Blackwell Publishing. I had no idea that I wanted to write this book, but after a conversation with her in early 2005, I knew exactly what I was going to write and why. Friends and colleagues read parts of the manuscript and offered encouragement as well as exceptionally astute advice. I am deeply grateful to Amanda Anderson, Michèle Barrett, Ben Bateman, Claire Colebrook, Kim Chabot Davis, Wai Chee Dimock, Susan Stanford Friedman, Heather Love, Janet Lyon, Gail McDonald, Jerome McGann, Toril Moi, Olga Taxidou, and Stephen White. Helpful reading suggestions came from Cristina Bruns and from virtually all my colleagues in the English department at the University of Virginia. Morgan Myers was an able research assistant. Allan Megill was a patient sounding board as well as a careful reader; many of his suggestions have found their way into my argument.

# Introduction

This is an odd manifesto as manifestos go, neither fish nor fowl, an awkward, ungainly creature that ill-fits its parentage. In one sense it conforms perfectly to type: one-sided, skew-eyed, it harps on one thing, plays only one note, gives one half of the story. Writing a manifesto is a perfect excuse for taking cheap shots, attacking straw men, and tossing babies out with the bath water. Yet the manifestos of the avant-garde were driven by the fury of their againstness, by an overriding impulse to slash and burn, to debunk and to demolish, to knock art off its pedestal and trample its shards into the dust. What follows is, in this sense, an un-manifesto: a negation of a negation, an act of yea-saying not nay-saying, a thought experiment that seeks to advocate, not denigrate.

There is a dawning sense among literary and cultural critics that a shape of thought has grown old. We know only too well the well-oiled machine of ideology critique, the x-ray gaze of symptomatic reading, the smoothly rehearsed moves that add up to a hermeneutics of suspicion. Ideas that seemed revelatory thirty years ago – the decentered subject! the social construction of reality! – have dwindled into shopworn slogans; defamiliarizing has lapsed into doxa, no less dogged and often as dogmatic as the certainties it sought to disrupt. And what virtue remains in the act of unmasking when we know full well what lies beneath the mask? More and more critics are venturing to ask what is lost when a dialogue with literature gives way to a permanent diagnosis, when the remedial reading of texts loses all sight of why we are drawn to such texts in the first place.

1

Our students, meanwhile, are migrating in droves toward vocationally oriented degrees in the hope of guaranteeing future incomes to offset sky-rocketing college bills. The institutional fiefdoms of the natural and social sciences pull in ever heftier sums of grant money and increasingly call the shots in the micro-dramas of university politics. In the media and public life, what counts as knowledge is equated with a piling up of data and graphs, questionnaires and pie charts, input-output ratios and feedback loops. Old-school beliefs that exposure to literature and art was a sure path to moral improvement and cultural refinement have fallen by the wayside, to no one's great regret. In such an austere and inauspicious climate, how do scholars of literature make a case for the value of what we do? How do we come up with rationales for reading and talking about books without reverting to the canon-worship of the past?

According to one line of thought, literary studies is entirely to blame for its own state of malaise. The rise of theory led to the death of literature, as works of art were buried under an avalanche of sociological sermons and portentous French prose. The logic of this particular accusation, however, is difficult to discern. Theory simply is the process of reflecting on the underlying frameworks, principles, and assumptions that shape our individual acts of interpretation. Championing literature against theory turns out to be a contradiction in terms, for those who leap to literature's defense must resort to their own generalities, conjectures, and speculative claims. Even as he sulks and pouts at theory's baleful effects, Harold Bloom's assertion that we read "in order to strengthen the self and learn its authentic interests" is a quintessential theoretical statement.[1]

Yet we can concede that the current canon of theory yields a paucity of rationales for attending to literary objects. We are called on to adopt poses of analytical detachment, critical vigilance, guarded suspicion; humanities scholars suffer from a terminal case of irony, driven by the uncontrollable urge to put everything in scare quotes. Problematizing, interrogating, and subverting are the default options, the deeply grooved patterns of contemporary thought. "Critical reading" is the holy grail of literary studies, endlessly

2

invoked in mission statements, graduation speeches, and conversations with deans, a slogan that peremptorily assigns all value to the act of reading and none to the objects read.[2] Are these objects really inert and indifferent, supine and submissive, entirely at the mercy of our critical maneuvers? Do we gain nothing in particular from what we read?

Literary theory has taught us that attending to the work itself is not a critical preference but a practical impossibility, that reading relies on a complex weave of presuppositions, expectations, and unconscious pre-judgments, that meaning and value are always assigned by someone, somewhere. And yet reading is far from being a one-way street; while we cannot help but impose ourselves on literary texts, we are also, inevitably, exposed to them. To elucidate the potential merits of such an exposure, rather than dwelling on its dangers, is to lay oneself open to charges of naïveté, boosterism, or metaphysical thinking. And yet, as teachers and scholars charged with advancing our discipline, we are sorely in need of more cogent and compelling justifications for what we do.

Eve Sedgwick observes that the hermeneutics of suspicion is now virtually de rigueur in literary theory, rather than one option among others. As a quintessentially paranoid style of critical engagement, it calls for constant vigilance, reading against the grain, assuming the worst-case scenario and then rediscovering its own gloomy prognosis in every text. (There is also something more than a little naïve, she observes, in the belief that the sheer gesture of exposing and demystifying ideas or images will somehow dissipate their effects.) Sedgwick's own suspicious reading of literary studies highlights the sheer strangeness of our taken-for-granted protocols of interpretation, the oddness of a critical stance so heavily saturated with negative emotion.[3] As I take it, Sedgwick is not lamenting any lack of sophisticated, formally conscious, even celebratory readings of literary works. Her point is rather that critics find themselves unable to justify such readings except by imputing to these works an intent to subvert, interrogate, or disrupt that mirrors their own. The negative has become inescapably, overbearingly, normative.

3

Moreover, even as contemporary theory prides itself on its exquisite self-consciousness, its relentless interrogation of fixed ideas, there is
a sense in which the very adoption of such a stance is pre-conscious
rather than freely made, choreographed rather than chosen, determined in advance by the pressure of institutional demands, intellectual
prestige, and the status-seeking protocols of professional advancement.
Which is simply to say that any savvy graduate student, when
faced with what looks like a choice between knowingness and
naïveté, will gravitate toward the former. This dichotomy, however,
will turn out to be false; knowing is far from synonymous with
knowingness, understood as a stance of permanent skepticism and
sharply honed suspicion. At this point, we are all resisting readers;
perhaps the time has come to resist the automatism of our own resistance, to risk alternate forms of aesthetic engagement.

This manifesto, then, vocalizes some reasons for reading while trying to steer clear of positions that are, in Sedgwick's words, "sappy,
aestheticizing, defensive, anti-intellectual, or reactionary."[4] It also strikes
a path away from the dominant trends of what I will call theological and ideological styles of reading. By "theological" I mean any
strong claim for literature's other-worldly aspects, though usually
in a secular rather than explicitly metaphysical sense. Simply put,
literature is prized for its qualities of otherness, for turning its back
on analytical and concept-driven styles of political or philosophical
thought as well as our everyday assumptions and commonsense beliefs.
We can find variations on such a stance in a wide range of critical
positions, including Harold Bloom's Romanticism, Kristeva's avant-
garde semiotics, and the current wave of Levinasian criticism. Such
perspectives differ drastically in their worldview, their politics, and
their methods of reading. What they share, nevertheless, is a conviction that literature is fundamentally different from the world
and our other ways of making sense of that world, and that this
difference – whether couched in the language of originality, singularity, alterity, untranslatability, or negativity – is the source of
its value.

At first glance, this argument sounds like an ideal solution to
the problem of justification. If we want to make a case for the

importance of something, what better way to do so than by show-casing its uniqueness? Indeed, it would be hard to dispute the claim that literary works yield signs of distinctiveness, difference, and otherness. We can surely sympathize with Marjorie Perloff's injunc-tion to respect an artwork's distinctive ontology rather than treating it as a confirmation of our own pet theories.[5] Yet this insight often comes at considerable cost. Separating literature from everything around it, critics fumble to explain how works of art arise from and move back into the social world. Highlighting literature's uniqueness, they overlook the equally salient realities of its connectedness. Applauding the ineffable and enigmatic qualities of works of art, they fail to do justice to the specific ways in which such works infiltrate and inform our lives. Faced with the disconcerting realization that people often turn to books for knowledge or entertainment, they can only lament the naïveté of those unable or unwilling to read literature "as literature." To read in such a way, it turns out, means assenting to a view of art as impervious to comprehension, assim-ilation, or real-world consequences, perennially guarded by a for-bidding "do not touch" sign, its value adjudicated by a culture of connoisseurship and a seminar-room sensibility anxious to ward off the grubby handprints and smears of everyday life. The case for literature's significance, it seems, can only be made by showcasing its impotence.

Some critics, I realize, would strenuously object to such a description, preferring to see the otherness of literature as a source of its radical and transformative potential. Thomas Docherty, for example, has recently crafted a vigorous defense of literary alterity as the necessary ground for a genuinely democratic politics – that is to say, a politics that calls for an ongoing confrontation with the unknown. The literary work enables an encounter with the extra-ordinary, an imagining of the impossible, an openness to pure other-ness, that is equipped with momentous political implications. There is certainly much to be said for the proposition that literature serves extra-aesthetic aims through its aesthetic features, yet these and similar claims for the radicalism of aesthetic form overlook those elements of familiarity, generic commonality, even predictability

5

that shape, however subtly, all literary texts, not to mention the routinization and professionalization of literary studies that must surely compromise any rhetoric of subversion. Moreover, the paean to the radical otherness of the literary text invariably turns out to be driven by an impatience with everyday forms of experience and less avant-garde forms of reading, which are peremptorily chastised for the crudity of their hermeneutic maneuvers. The singularity of literature, it turns out, can only be secured by the homogenizing and lumping together of everything else.[6]

Those critics drawn to the concept of ideology, by contrast, seek to place literature squarely in the social world. They insist that a text is always part of something larger; they highlight literature's relationship to what it is not. Hence the tactical role of the concept of ideology, as a way of signaling a relation to a broader social whole. Yet this same idea also has the less happy effect of rendering the work of art secondary or supernumerary, a depleted resource deficient in insights that must be supplied by the critic. Whatever definition of ideology is being deployed (and I am aware that the term has undergone a labyrinthine history of twists and turns), its use implies that a text is being diagnosed rather than heard, relegated to the status of a symptom of social structures or political causes. The terms of interpretation are set elsewhere; the work is barred from knowing what the critic knows; it remains blind to its own collusion in oppressive social circumstances. Lennard Davis, in one of the most forceful expressions of the literature-as-ideology school, insists that the role of fiction is to shore up the status quo, to guard against radical aspirations, and ultimately to pull the wool over readers' eyes.[7] Yet even those critics who abjure any notion of false consciousness, who deem the condition of being in ideology to be eternal and inescapable, impute to their own analyses a grasp of social circumstance inherently more perspicacious than the text's own.

Of course, the notion of ideology can also be applied in a laudatory, if slightly altered, sense, to hail a work's affinity with feminism, or Marxism, or struggles against racism. Literature, in this view, is open to recruitment as a potential medium of political enlightenment and social transformation. Yet the difficulty of secondariness, indeed subordination, remains: the literary text is hauled in to confirm what the critic already knows, to illustrate what has been adjudicated in other arenas. My intent is not at all to minimize the value of asking political questions of works of art, but to ask what is lost when we deny a work any capacity to bite back, in Ellen Rooney's phrase, to challenge or change our own beliefs and commitments.[8] To define literature as ideology is to have decided ahead of time that literary works can be objects of knowledge but never sources of knowledge. It is to rule out of court the eventuality that a literary text could know as much, or more, than a theory.

The current critical scene thus yields contrasting convictions on literature, value, and use. Ideological critics insist that works of literature, as things of this world, are always caught up in social hierarchies and struggles over power. The value of a text simply is its use, as measured by its role in either obscuring or accentuating social antagonisms. To depict art as apolitical or purposeless is simply, as Brecht famously contended, to ally oneself with the status quo. Theologically minded critics wince at such arguments, which they abjure as painfully reductive, wreaking violence on the qualities of aesthetic objects. Close at hand lies a deep reservoir of mistrust toward the idea of use; to measure the worth of something in terms of its utility, in this view, involves an alienating reduction of means to ends. Such mistrust can be voiced in many different registers: the language of Romantic aesthetics, the neo-Marxist critique of instrumental reason, the poststructuralist suspicion of identity thinking. What distinguishes literature, in this line of thought, is its obdurate resistance to all calculations of purpose and function.

By calling my book "uses of literature," I seem to have cast my lot with ideological criticism. In fact, I want to argue for an expanded understanding of "use" – one that offers an alternative to either strong claims for literary otherness or the whittling down of texts to the bare bones of political and ideological function. Such a notion of use allows us to engage the worldly aspects of literature in a way that is respectful rather than reductive, dialogic rather than high-handed. "Use" is not always strategic or purposeful, manipulative or grasping; it does not have to involve the sway of instrumental rationality or a willful blindness to complex form. I venture that aesthetic value is inseparable from use, but also that our engagements with texts are extraordinarily varied, complex, and often unpredictable in kind. The pragmatic, in this sense, neither destroys not excludes the poetic. To propose that the meaning of literature lies in its use is to open up for investigation a vast terrain of practices, expectations, emotions, hopes, dreams, and interpretations – a terrain that is, in William James's words, "multitudinous beyond imagination, tangled, muddy, painful and perplexed."[9]

I am always bemused, in this context, to hear critics assert that literary works serve no evident purpose, even as their engagement with such works patently showcases their critical talents, gratifies their intellectual and aesthetic interests, and, in the crassest sense, furthers their careers. How can art ever exist outside a many-sided play of passions and purposes? Conversely, those anxious to locate literature's essential qualities in well-defined ideological agendas lay themselves open to methodological objections of various stripes. It is not that such critics overlook form in favor of theme and content, as conservatives like to complain; schooled by decades of semiotics and poststructuralist theory, they are often scrupulously alert to nuances of language, structure, and style. Difficulties arise, however, when critics try to force an equivalence of textual structures with social structures, to assert a necessary causality between literary forms and larger political effects. In this context, we see frequent attempts to endow literary works with what Amanda Anderson calls aggrandized agency, to portray them as uniquely powerful objects, able to single-handedly impose coercive regimes of power or to unleash insurrectionary surges of resistance.[10]

In some cases, to be sure, literary works can boast a measurable social impact. In my first book, I made what I still find a plausible case for the role of feminist fiction of the 1970s and 1980s in altering political and cultural attitudes and creating what I called a counter-public sphere. But when we look at many of the works that literary critics like to read, it is often far from self-evident what role such works play in either initiating or inhibiting social change. Stripped

8

of any direct links to oppositional movements, marked by often uneasy relations to centers of power, their politics are revealed as oblique and equivocal, lending themselves to alternative, even antithetical readings. Texts, furthermore, lack the power to legislate their own effects; the internal features of a literary work tell us little about how it is received and understood, let alone its impact, if any, on a larger social field. Political function cannot be deduced or derived from literary structure. As cultural studies and reception studies have amply shown, aesthetic objects may acquire very different meanings in altered contexts; the transactions between texts and readers are varied, contingent, and often unpredictable.

None of this, perhaps, sounds especially new or controversial. Aren't many of us trying to weave our way between the Scylla of political functionalism and the Charybdis of art for art's sake, striving to do justice to the social meanings of artworks without slighting their aesthetic power? One of the happier consequences of the historical turn in criticism has been the crafting of more flexible and finely tuned accounts of how literature is embedded in the world. Ato Quayson offers one such account in describing the literary work as a form of aesthetic particularity that is also a threshold, opening out onto other levels of cultural and sociopolitical life.[11] I am also thinking of my own field, feminist criticism, which has stringently reassessed many of its arguments over recent years. Rather than imputing an invariant kernel of feminist or misogynist content to literary texts, critics nowadays are more inclined to highlight their mutating and conflicting meanings. A heightened attentiveness to the details of milieu and moment and to the multifarious ways in which gender and literature interconnect allows such readings to withstand the charges of reductionism that can be leveled at more sweeping theories of social context.

Such historically attuned approaches strike me as infinitely more fruitful than the attempt to force a union between aesthetics and politics, to write as if literary forms or genres bear within them an essential and inviolable ideological core. Taking their cue from Foucault, they circumvent the problem of secondariness by treating literary texts as formative in their own right, as representations that summon up new ways of seeing rather than as echoes or distortions of predetermined political truths. Espousing what cultural studies calls a politics of articulation, they show how the meanings of texts change as they hook up with different interests and interpretive communities. Moreover, such neo-historical approaches have also shown a willingness to attend to the affective aspects of reading, to ponder the distinctive qualities of particular structures of feeling, and to recover, through their engagement with forms such as melodrama and the sentimental novel, lost histories of aesthetic response.[12]

Yet every method has its sins of omission as well as commission, things that it is simply unable to see or do. As a method, we might say, historical criticism encourages a focus on the meanings of texts *for others*: the work is anchored at its point of origin, defined in relation to a past interplay of interests and forces, discourses and audiences. Of course, every critic nowadays recognizes that we can never hope to recreate the past "as it really was," that our vision of history is propelled, at least in part, by the desires and needs of the present. Yet interpretation still pivots around a desire to capture, as adequately as possible, the cultural sensibility of a past moment, and literature's meaning in that moment.

One consequence of such historical embedding is that the critic is absolved of the need to think through her own relationship to the text she is reading. Why has this work been chosen for interpretation? How does it speak to me now? What is its value in the present? To focus only on a work's origins is to side-step the question of its appeal to the present-day reader. It is, in a Nietzschean sense, to use history as an alibi, a way of circumventing the question of one's own attachments, investments, and vulnerabilities as a reader. The text cannot speak, insofar as it is already spoken for by an accumulation of historical evidence. Yet the cumulative force of its past associations, connotations, and effects by no means exhausts a work's power of address. What of its ability to traverse temporal boundaries and to generate new and unanticipated resonances, including those that cannot be predicted by its original circumstances? Our conventional modes of historical criticism, observes Wai Chee Dimock, "cannot say why this text might still matter in the present, why, distanced from its original period, it nonetheless continues to signify, continues to invite other readings."[13]

Such questions become especially salient when we venture beyond the sphere of academic criticism. Most readers, after all, have no interest in the fine points of literary history; when they pick up a book from the past, they do so in the hope that it will speak to them in the present. And the teaching of literature in schools and universities still pivots, in the last analysis, around an individual encounter with a text. While students nowadays are likely to be informed about critical debates and literary theories, they are still expected to find their own way into a literary work, not to parrot the interpretations of others. What, then, is the nature of that encounter? What intellectual or affective responses are involved? Any attempt to clarify the value of literature must surely engage the diverse motives of readers and ponder the mysterious event of reading, yet contemporary theories give us poor guidance on such questions. We are sorely in need of richer and deeper accounts of how selves interact with texts.

To be sure, it is axiomatic nowadays that interpretation is never neutral or objective, but always shaped by what critics like to call the reader's "subject position." Yet the models of selfhood on hand in contemporary criticism suffer from an overly schematic imperative, as critics strain to calculate the relative impact exercised by pressures of gender, race, sexuality, and the like, in order to recruit literature in the drama of asserting or subverting such categories. The making and unmaking of identity, however, while a theme much loved by contemporary critics, is not a rubric well equipped to capture the sheer thickness of subjectivity or the mutability of aesthetic response.[14] Nor is psychoanalysis, with its built-in machinery of diagnosis and causal explanation, especially well suited for fine-grained descriptions of the affective attachments and cognitive reorientations that characterize the experience of reading a book or watching a film. The issue here is by no means one of evading or transcending the political; rather, any "textual politics" worth its weight will have to work its way through the particularities of aesthetic experience rather than bypassing them.

11

In this regard, John Guillory helps us to see that what look like political disagreements often say more about the schism between academic criticism and lay reading. Scholarly reading, he points out, is an activity shaped by distinctive conditions and expectations. It is a form of *work*, compensated for by salary and other forms of recognition; it is a *disciplinary activity* governed by conventions of interpretation and research developed over decades; it espouses *vigilance*, standing back from the pleasure of reading to encourage critical reflection; it is a *communal practice*, subject to the judgment of other professional readers. Guillory's point is not at all to lament or bemoan these facts, which have allowed literary study to define and sustain itself as a scholarly field. It is rather to underscore that they exercise an intense, if often invisible, pressure on the day-to-day practice of literary critics, however avant-garde or politically progressive they claim to be. The ethos of academic reading diverges significantly from lay reading; the latter is a leisure activity, it is shaped by differing conventions of interpretation, it is undertaken voluntarily and for pleasure, and is often a solitary practice.[15] The failure to acknowledge the implications of these differences goes a long way toward explaining the communicative mishaps between scholars of literature and the broader public. That one person immerses herself in the joys of *Jane Eyre*, while another views it as a symptomatic expression of Victorian imperialism, often has less to do with the political beliefs of those involved than their position in different scenes of readings.

As Guillory acknowledges, this distinction is not a dichotomy; professional critics were once lay readers, after all, while the tenets of academic criticism often filter down, via the classroom, to larger audiences. Yet literary theorists patrol the boundaries of their field with considerable alacrity and enthusiasm. Take, for example, the idea of recognition: the widespread belief that we learn something about ourselves in the act of reading. Theological criticism responds with alarm, insisting that any act of recognition cannot help but do violence to the alterity of the literary work. Ideological criticism is equally censorious, insisting that any apparent recognition be demoted without further ado to an instance of misrecognition. Both styles of criticism, we should note, are propelled by a deep-seated discomfort with everyday language and thought, a conviction that commonsense beliefs exist only to be unmasked and found wanting.

It is here that I would stake a claim for the distinctiveness of my argument. Rather than pitting literary theory against common knowledge, I hope to build better bridges between them. This is not because I endorse every opinion expressed in the name of common sense – quite the contrary – but because theoretical reflection is powered by, and indebted to, many of the same motives and structures that shape everyday thinking, so that any disavowal of such thinking must reek of bad faith. In retrospect, much of the grand theory of the last three decades now looks like the last gasp of an Enlightenment tradition of *rois philosophes* persuaded that the realm of speculative thought would absolve them of the shameful ordinariness of a messy, mundane, error-prone existence. Moreover, the various jeremiads against commodification, carceral regimes of power, and the tyranny of received ideas and naturalized ideologies mesh all too comfortably with an ingrained Romantic tradition of anti-worldliness in literary studies. In idealizing an autonomous, difficult art as the only source of resistance to such repressive regimes, they also shortchange the heterogeneous, and politically variable, uses of literary texts in daily life.[16]

What follows is in this sense the quintessential un-manifesto; it demurs from the vanguardist sensibility that continues to characterize much literary theory, even as the concept of the avant-garde has lost much of its credibility. There is no compelling reason why the practice of theory requires us to go behind the backs of ordinary persons in order to expose their beliefs as deluded or delinquent. Indeed, the contemporary intellectual scene also yields an assortment of traditions – pragmatism, cultural studies, Habermasian theory, ordinary language philosophy – that address the limits of scholarly skepticism and that conceive of everyday thinking as an indispensable resource rather than a zone of dull compulsion and self-deception.[17] What would it mean to take this idea and place it at the heart of literary theory?

13

Among other things, it calls on us to engage seriously with ordinary motives for reading – such as the desire for knowledge or the longing for escape – that are either overlooked or undervalued in literary scholarship. While rarely acknowledged, however, such motives also retain a shadowy presence among the footnotes and fortifications of academic prose. The use of the term "reading" in literary studies to encompass quite disparate activities, from turning the pages of a paperback novel to elaborate exegeses published in *PMLA*, glosses over their many differences. The latter reading constitutes a writing, a public performance subject to a host of gate-keeping practices and professional norms: a premium on novelty and deft displays of counter-intuitive interpretive ingenuity, the obligation to reference key scholars in the field, rapidly changing critical vocabularies, and the tacit prohibition of certain stylistic registers. This practice often has little in common with the commentary a teacher carries out in the classroom, or with what goes through her mind when she reads a book in an armchair, at home. Published academic criticism, in other words, is not an especially reliable or comprehensive guide to the ways in which academics read. We are less theoretically pure than we think ourselves to be; hard-edged poses of suspicion and skepticism jostle against more mundane yet more variegated responses. My argument is not a populist defense of folk reading over scholarly interpretation, but an elucidation of how, in spite of their patent differences, they share certain affective and cognitive parameters.

In the following pages, I proposes that reading involves a logic of *recognition*; that aesthetic experience has analogies with *enchantment* in a supposedly disenchanted age; that literature creates distinctive configurations of social *knowledge*; that we may value the experience of being *shocked* by what we read. These four categories epitomize what I call modes of textual engagement: they are neither intrinsic literary properties nor independent psychological states, but denote multi-leveled interactions between texts and readers that are irreducible to their separate parts. Such modes of engagement are woven into modern histories of self-formation and transformation, even as the very variability of their uses militates against a calculus that would pare them down to a single political purpose.

Readers will detect in these terms the shadowy presence of some venerable aesthetic categories (anagnorisis, beauty, mimesis, the sublime), to which I hope nevertheless to give a fresh spin. These four categories are obviously neither exhaustive nor mutually exclusive: I separate for the sake of analytical clarity strands of aesthetic response that are frequently intertwined and even interfused. But I hold fast to the view that any account of why people read must operate on several different fronts, that we should relinquish, once and for all, the pursuit of a master concept, a key to all the mythologies. As soon as critics insist that the role of literature really is to inspire aesthetic rapture, or to encourage moral reflection and self-scrutiny, or to act as a force-field transforming relations of power, it is all too easy to come up with countless examples of forms or genres that do the exact opposite.

While ordinary intuitions are a valuable starting point for reflecting on why literature matters, it is far from self-evident what such intuitions signify. The mundane, on closer inspection, often turns out to be exceptionally mysterious. The purpose of literary criticism, if it has any pretension to being a scholarly field, cannot be to echo what non-academic readers already know. A respect for everyday perceptions is entirely compatible with a commitment to theory; such perceptions give us questions to pursue, not answers. What follows bears little relationship, I hope, to the strain of anti-intellectualism that animates literary studies in its darkest hours, the surrendering to intuition, charisma, and an all-encompassing love of literature.

I also dissent from some recent reclamations of aesthetic experiences that champion the affective over the rational, the sensual over the conceptual, and intrinsic over extrinsic meaning. I retain enough of my sociological convictions to believe that aesthetic pleasure is never unmediated or intrinsic, that even our most inchoate and seemingly ineffable responses are shaped by dispositions transmitted through education and culture. I am also not persuaded that justifying the value of aesthetic experience requires a full-scale

15

repudiation of conceptual or political thought. The pleasures of literature are often tied up with epistemic gains and insights into our social being, insights that are rooted in, rather than at odds with, its distinctive uses and configurations of language. My aim is to give equal weight to cognitive and affective aspects of aesthetic response; any theory worth its salt surely needs to ponder how literature changes our understanding of ourselves and the world as well as its often visceral impact on our psyche.[18]

My argument also injects a modest dose of phenomenology into current theoretical debates. I refer to phenomenology with a degree of trepidation; as far as I can tell, my approach has very little in common with Husserl or the Geneva school. Nor have I found much guidance in the phenomenological wing of reader-response theory; while scholars like Wolfgang Iser and Roman Ingarden usefully highlight the interactive nature of reading, they assume a highly formalist model of aesthetic response as a universal template for talking about how readers respond to books. Their imagined readers are curiously bloodless and disembodied, stripped of all passions as well as of ethical or political commitments. They conform, in other words, to a notably one-sided ideal of the academic or professional reader. I simply do not share the view that formal ambiguity, irony, and the unsettling of familiar schemata are always the highest aesthetic values and the only reasons why we look to literary texts.

Nor do I buy into the idea of what phenomenologists like to call transcendental reduction, the attempt to strip off the surface accouterments of cultural and historical difference in order to access a core subjectivity. We cannot shrug off our prejudices, beliefs and assumptions; self and society are always interfused; there is no clear place where one ends and the other begins. Subjectivity is always caught up with intersubjectivity, personal experience awash with social and political meanings. I concur with Ricoeur's recasting of phenomenology as the interpretation of symbols rather than the intuition of essences, as well as his insistence that the self is always already another, formed at its core through the mediating force of stories, metaphors, myths and images. My approach, like Ricoeur's, is best

16

described as an impure or hybrid phenomenology that latches onto, rather than superseding, my historical commitments.

What I find valuable about phenomenology is its attentiveness to the first person perspective, to the ways in which phenomena disclose themselves to the self. Phenomenology insists that the world is always the world as it appears to us, as it is filtered through our consciousness, perception, and judgment. We can learn to question our own beliefs; we can come to see that our seemingly spontaneous reactions are shaped by cultural pressures; we can acknowledge, in short, the historicity of our experience. And yet we cannot vault outside our own vantage point, as the inescapable and insuperable condition for our being in the world. Phenomenology encourages us to zoom in and look closely at what this condition of being-a-self involves. Such scrutiny, it seems to me, does not require any belief in the autonomy or wholeness of persons, nor a disavowal of the obscurity or opacity of aspects of consciousness. Everyday attitudes are neither invalidated (as they are in poststructuralism and much political criticism) nor are they taken as self-explanatory (as in humanist criticism, with its unexamined use of terms such as "self" or "value"); rather they become worthy of investigation in all their many-sidedness. Thus the titles of my chapters name quite ordinary structures of experience that are also political, philosophical, and aesthetic concepts fanning out into complex histories.

How can such an injection of phenomenology deepen our sense of the aesthetics and politics of the literary text? "Back to the things themselves" was phenomenology's famous rallying cry: the insistence that we need to learn to see – to really see – what lies right under our noses. We are called on, in other words, to do justice to how readers respond to the words they encounter, rather than relying on textbook theories or wishful speculations about what reading is supposed to be. The Kantian legacy has not been helpful here: Kant was intent on developing a theory of natural beauty rather than a full-blown definition of art, and subsequent interpretations of his ideas have encouraged a misleading conflation of the aesthetic with the artistic.[19] The mode of perception valued by Kantians – a single-minded attention to form, beauty, or expressive design that is

17

conventionally called "aesthetic" – is one possible response to art-works, but hardly an essential or exclusive one. This is not at all to deny that art attains a degree of autonomy in modernity, but to under-score that this process is more uneven, ambivalent, conflictual, and qualified than is often acknowledged. A phenomenology of reading calls for an undogmatic openness to a spectrum of literary responses; that some of these responses are not currently sanctioned in the annals of professional criticism does not render them any less salient.

Moreover, a dose of phenomenology allows for a notably less wish-ful account of the political work that texts can do. Literary critics love to assign exceptional powers to the texts they read, to write as if the rise of the novel were single-handedly responsible for the formation of bourgeois subjects or to assume that subversive currents of social agitation will flow, as if by fiat, from their favorite piece of performance art. Texts, however, are unable to act directly on the world, but only via the intercession of those who read them. These readers are heterogeneous and complex microcosms: socially sculpted yet internally regulated complexes of beliefs and sentiments, of patterns of inertia and impulses toward innovation, of cultural com-monalities interwoven with quirky predispositions. In the two-way transaction we call reading, texts pass through densely woven filters of interpretation and affective orientation that both enable and limit their impact. Zooming in to scrutinize the many-sided and multiply determined act of reading cannot help but reveal that the effects of literature are neither as transfigurative as aesthetes like to claim nor as ruthlessly authoritarian as some radicals want to insist.

This book, then, contributes to a neo-phenomenology that blends historical and phenomenological perspectives, that respects the intri-cacy and complexity of consciousness without shelving sociopolitical reflection. Steven Connor has been a pioneer in this new phenom-enological turn, arguing for closer attention to those "substances, habits, organs, rituals, obsessions, pathologies, processes and pat-terns of feeling" that are occluded by the usual frameworks of critical theory as well as by formalist invocations of literariness.[20] The current surge of interest in emotion and affect across a range of disciplinary fields contributes to an intellectual climate notably more receptive to thick descriptions of experiential states. Queer theory also comes to mind as a field that is acquiring a phenomenological flavor: inspired by Sedgwick's afore-mentioned critique of a hermeneutics of suspicion, critics are delving into the eddies and flows of affective engagement, trying to capture something of the quality and the sheer intensity of attachments and orientations rather than rushing to explain them, judge them, or wish them away.[21]

For some readers, no doubt, any hint of phenomenology will seem too crassly unhistorical, too blind to cultural specifics, so that it may be helpful to elaborate on the delicate equilibrium of commonality and difference, of theory and history. The aesthetic responses I discuss owe much to the conditions of modernity, when reading comes to assume a new and formative role in the shaping of selfhood. I hazard no claims whatsoever about structures of thought and feeling that govern pre-modern or non-modern forms of reading. While circling around these modes of literary engagement, I strive to remain mindful of the pressures of social and historical circumstance as they inflect aesthetic response. While there are differences in how modern readers experience shock or recognition, however, there are also continuities – those very continuities that make it possible to recognize a particular Gestalt, a distinctive structure of thought or feeling. There is much to be said for attending to these continuities in the context of a critical history that has paid scant attention to their distinctive features and internal complexities as modes of aesthetic engagement. I want to ponder what it means to be enchanted as well as to document particular episodes of enchantment.

There are also times when the act of historicizing can harden into a defense mechanism, a means of holding an artwork at arm's length. We quantify and qualify, hesitate and complicate, surround texts with dense thickets of historical description and empirical detail, distancing them as firmly as possible from our own threateningly inchoate, or theoretically incorrect, desires and investments. In this sense phenomenology offers a worthy complement and ally, rather than an opponent, to such acts of embedding. If historical analysis takes place in the third person, phenomenology ties such analysis back to the first person, clarifying how and why particular texts matter to us. We are called on to honor our implication and involvement in the works we read, rather than serving as shame-faced bystanders to our own aesthetic response. Here my argument links up with a recent ethical turn in literary studies, an exhortation to look at, rather than through, the literary work, to attend to the act of saying rather than only the substance of what is said. The act of reading enacts an ethics and a politics in its own right, rather than being a displacement of something more essential that is taking place elsewhere.[22]

In this context, I find myself drawn toward the idea of "emphatic experience," a phrase that can do justice to the differential force and intensity of aesthetic encounters without subscribing to essentialist dichotomies of high versus low art.[23] The last few decades have inspired blistering critiques of canonicity and traditional value hierarchies. Yet such critiques often lapse back into an antiquated and thoroughly discredited positivism in assuming that the problem of value can simply be eliminated. In fact, as their own arguments all too clearly demonstrate, evaluation is not optional: we are condemned to choose, required to rank, endlessly engaged in practices of selecting, sorting, distinguishing, privileging, whether in academia or in everyday life. We need only look at the texts we elect to interpret, the works we include in our syllabi, or the theories we deign to approve, ignore, or condemn. The critique of value merely underscores the persistence of evaluation in the very act of assigning a negative judgment. As John Frow remarks, "there is no escape from the discourse of value," which is neither intrinsic to the object nor forged single-handedly by a subject, but arises out of a complex interplay between institutional structures, interpretive communities, and the idiosyncrasies of individual taste.[24]

Values vary, of course, in literature as in life. Someone who praises a novel for its searingly honest depiction of the everyday lives of Icelandic fishermen is appealing to a different framework of value than another reader who lauds the same text for its subversive aesthetic of self-shattering. The following pages make a case for the variability, and in some cases the incommensurability, of value frameworks. Even within a specific framework of value, moreover, judgments differ. While aesthetic preferences are influenced by social cleavages and cultural pressures, they bear no simple or direct expressive relationship to a particular political demographic or collectivity. In this sense, attempts to circumscribe the features of a female aesthetic, a popular aesthetic, or a black aesthetic, to cite a few recent examples, are inevitably stymied by the variability of both value judgments and value frameworks within a particular social grouping.

The idea of "emphatic experience" is capacious enough to contain multiple value frameworks while also honoring the differential nature of our responses to specific texts. It acknowledges that our attachments differ in degree and in kind, that we do not and cannot favor all texts equally, that in any given assortment of tragedies or TV dramas we are guaranteed to find some examples more memorable, more compelling, simply more extraordinary than others. Yet by leaving open the nature and content of that emphatic experience, as well as the criteria used to evaluate it, it grants the sheer range of aesthetic response: individuals can be moved by different texts for very different reasons. This insight has often been lost to literary studies, thanks to a single-minded fixation on the merits of irony, ambiguity, and indeterminacy that leaves it mystified by other structures of value and fumbling to make sense of alternative responses to works of art.

In this regard, one advantage – or stumbling block, depending on your viewpoint – of what follows is that it canvasses ways of thinking about aesthetic experience that do not hinge on the presumed superiority of literature or literariness. My focus on novels, plays, and poems derives from my own training and limited expertise; departments of literature, moreover, are especially hard hit by a legitimation crisis that is affecting all of the humanities. Yet much of what I have to say also pertains to art forms such as film, which are assuming an increasingly vital role as purveyors of epistemic insights, vocabularies of self-understanding, and affective states (I touch most explicitly on film in chapter two). If literary studies is to survive the twenty-first century, it will need to reinvigorate its ambitions and its methods by forging closer links to the study of other media rather than clinging to ever more tenuous claims to exceptional status. Such collaborations will require, of course, scrupulous attention to the medium-specific features of artistic forms.

What follows, then, is a gamble, a perhaps quixotic wager that a one-sided reflection on literature will allow its many dimensions to unfold. The last few decades have molded us into skeptical readers, forever on our guard against the hidden agendas of aesthetic forms. Even when critics strain for a measure of even-handedness, texts are all too often shoe-horned into a rudimentary dialectic of coercion versus freedom, containment versus transgression, such that the distinctive modalities of aesthetic experience are shortchanged. I offer, instead, a thought experiment, an attempt to see things from another angle, to rough out, if you will, the shape of a positive aesthetics. When skepticism has become routinized, self-protective, even reassuring, it is time to become suspicious of our entrenched suspicions, to question the confidence of our own diagnostic authority, and to face up, once and for all, to the force of our attachments.

The point is not to abandon the tools we have honed, the insights we have gained; we cannot, in any event, return to a state of innocence, or ignorance. In the long run, we should all heed Ricoeur's advice to combine a willingness to suspect with an eagerness to listen; there is no reason why our readings cannot blend analysis and attachment, criticism and love. In recent years, however, the pendulum has lurched entirely too far in one direction; our language of critique is far more sophisticated and substantial than our language of justification. For the span of a few pages, I plan to pursue an alternative line of thought and err in a different direction. Is it possible to discuss the value of literature without falling into truisms and platitudes, sentimentality and *Schwärmerei*? Let us see.

# 1

## *Recognition*

What does it mean to recognize oneself in a book? The experience seems at once utterly mundane yet singularly mysterious. While turning a page I am arrested by a compelling description, a constellation of events, a conversation between characters, an interior monologue. Suddenly and without warning, a flash of connection leaps across the gap between text and reader; an affinity or an attunement is brought to light. I may be looking for such a moment, or I may stumble on it haphazardly, startled by the prescience of a certain combination of words. In either case, I feel myself addressed, summoned, called to account: I cannot help seeing traces of myself in the pages I am reading. Indisputably, something has changed; my perspective has shifted; I see something that I did not see before.

Novels yield up manifold descriptions of such moments of readjustment, as fictional readers are wrenched out of their circumstances by the force of written words. Think of Thomas Buddenbrook opening up the work of Schopenhauer and being intoxicated by a system of ideas that casts his life in a bewildering new light. Or Stephen Gordon, in *The Well of Loneliness*, stunned to discover that her desire to be a man and love a woman is not without precedent after stumbling across the works of Krafft-Ebing in her father's library. Such episodes show readers becoming absorbed in scripts that confound their sense of who and what they are. They come to see themselves differently by gazing outward rather than inward, by deciphering ink marks on a page.

Often it is a work of fiction that triggers fervent self-scrutiny. *The Picture of Dorian Gray* describes Dorian's infatuation with a book that is usually assumed to be J. K. Huysmans' decadent manifesto, *Against Nature*. "The hero, the wonderful young Parisian, in whom the romantic and the scientific temperaments were so strangely blended, became to him a kind of prefiguring type of himself. And, indeed, the whole book seemed to him to contain the story of his own life, written before he had lived it."[1] Here recognition is not retrospective but anticipatory: the fictional work foreshadows what Dorian will become, the potential that lies dormant but has not yet come to light. And a hundred years later, the young narrator of Pankaj Mishra's novel *The Romantics*, a student living in Benares, develops an obsession with Flaubert's *Sentimental Education*, noting that "the protagonist, Frédéric Moreau, seemed to mirror my own self-image with his large, passionate, but imprecise longings, his indecisiveness, his aimlessness, his self-contempt."[2] Interleaving Flaubert's words with his own, Mishra writes back to those who would indict canonical texts for turning Indians into would-be Europeans, suggesting that a more intricate and multi-layered encounter is taking place.

These vignettes of recognition, to be sure, are plucked from disparate, even disjunctive, literary worlds. *The Well of Loneliness* leaves its readers in no doubt that a momentous discovery has taken place; whatever our view of sexology, we are asked to believe that Stephen Gordon has arrived at a crucial insight about her place in the world. An impasse has been breached, something has been laid bare, a truth has been uncovered. Elsewhere, the moment of recognition is so thickly leavened with irony as to leave us uncertain whether self-knowledge has been gained or lost. Does Dorian come to fathom something of his deepest inclinations and desires, or is he simply seduced by the glamor of a fashionable book, lured into imitating an imitation in an endless hall of mirrors? Surely this particular moment of self-apprehension is thorough qualified by Wilde's own leanings towards theatricality and artifice, his rendering of Dorian as a pastiche of the desires and words of others. And yet, if we, as readers, are made aware of a more general impressionability and susceptibility to imitation through Dorian's response, has an act of recognition not nevertheless taken place?

Taken together, these examples point to the perplexing and paradoxical nature of recognition. Simultaneously reassuring and unnerving, it brings together likeness and difference in one fell swoop. When we recognize something, we literally "know it again"; we make sense of what is unfamiliar by fitting it into an existing scheme, linking it to what we already know. Yet, as Gadamer points out, "the joy of recognition is rather the joy of knowing *more* than is already familiar."[3] Recognition is not repetition; it denotes not just the previously known, but the becoming known. Something that may have been sensed in a vague, diffuse, or semi-conscious way now takes on a distinct shape, is amplified, heightened, or made newly visible. In a mobile interplay of exteriority and interiority, something that exists outside of me inspires a revised or altered sense of who I am.

That the novel should brood over its own effects is far from surprising, given its intimate and intricate implication in the history of the self. One of its most persistent plots describes a hero launching himself on a process of self-exploration while puzzling over what shape and form his life should take. For Charles Taylor and Anthony Giddens, this idea of selfhood as an unfolding and open-ended project, what Taylor calls the impulse toward self-fashioning, crystallizes a distinctively modern sense of identity. Cut loose from the bonds of tradition and rigid social hierarchies, individuals are called to the burdensome freedom of choreographing their life and endowing it with a purpose. As selfhood becomes self-reflexive, literature comes to assume a crucial role in exploring what it means to be a person. The novel, especially, embraces a heightened psychological awareness, meditating on the murky depths of motive and desire, seeking to map the elusive currents and by-ways of consciousness, highlighting countless connections and conflicts between self-determination and socialization. Depicting characters engaged in introspection and soul-searching, it encourages its readers to engage in similar acts of self-scrutiny. It speaks to a distinctively modern sense of individuality – what one critic calls improvisational subjectivity – yet this very conviction of personal uniqueness and interior depth is infused by the ideas of others.[4] One learns how to be oneself by taking one's cue from others who are doing the same. From the tormented effusions of young Werther to the elegiac reflections of Mrs. Dalloway, the novel spins out endless modulations on the theme of subjectivity.

Cultural history as well as casual conversation suggest that recognition is a common event while reading and a powerful motive for reading. Proust famously observes that

> every reader is, while he is reading, the reader of his own self. The writer's work is merely a kind of optical instrument which he offers to the reader to enable him to discern what, without this book, he would perhaps never have perceived himself. And the recognition by the reader in his own self of what the book says is the proof of its veracity.[5]

This coupling of reading with self-scrutiny has acquired renewed vigor and intensity in recent decades, as women and minorities found literature an especially pertinent medium for parsing the complexities of personhood. And yet, even as recognition pervades practices of reading and interpretation, theoretical engagement with recognition is hedged round with prohibitions and taboos, often spurned as unseemly, even shameful, seen as the equivalent of a suicidal plunge into unprofessional naïveté. Isn't it the ultimate form of narcissism to think that a book is really about me? Isn't there something excruciatingly self-serving about reading a literary work as an allegory of one's own dilemmas and personal difficulties? And don't we risk trivializing and limiting the realm of art once we start turning texts into mirrors of ourselves?

This wariness of recognition has been boosted by the recent impact of Levinas on literary studies. As an advocate of otherness, Levinas warns against the hubris of thinking that we can ultimately come to understand that which is different or strange. Ethics means accepting the mysteriousness of the other, its resistance to conceptual schemes; it means learning to relinquish our own desire to know. Seeking to link a literary work to one's own life is a threat to its irreducible singularity. For theorists weaned on the language of alterity and difference, the mere mention of recognition is likely to inspire raised eyebrows. To recognize is not just to trivialize but also to colonize; it is a sign of narcissistic self-duplication, a scandalous solipsism, an imperious expansion of a subjectivity that seeks to appropriate otherness by turning everything into a version of itself.

If the idea of recognition is acknowledged at all in literary theory, it is to be alchemized – via the reagent of Lacan or Althusser – into a state of misrecognition. We owe to these thinkers two celebrated fables of self-deception. Lacan's essay on the mirror stage conjures up the scenario of a small child gazing into the mirror, mesmerized by his own image. Thanks to the reflecting power of a glass surface – or the encouraging, imitative gestures of the mother-as-mirror – he comes to acquire a nascent sense of self. What was previously inchoate starts to coalesce into a unity as the child realizes that he is that image reflected back by the sheen of the mirror. Yet this moment of recognition is illusory, the first of many such moments of misapprehension. Not only does the image of the self originate outside the self, but the seemingly substantial figure that looks back from the mirror belies the void that lies at the heart of identity. Lacan's subject is essentially hollow, a spectral figure that epitomizes the sheer impossibility of ever knowing the self.

For Althusser, the seminal instance of misrecognition takes place on the street, at the moment of what he calls interpellation or hailing. As I am walking along, I hear a police officer calling out "hey, you there!" somewhere behind me. In the very act of turning around, of feeling myself addressed by this generic summons, I am created as a subject. I acknowledge my existence as an individual, as someone bound by the law. To recognize oneself as a subject is to thus to accede to one's own subjection; the self believes itself to be free yet is everywhere in chains. One's personhood has a sheer obviousness about it as a self-evident reality that demands to be recognized. Yet this very obviousness renders it the essence of ideology, the quintessential means by which politics does its work. It is via the snare of a fictional subjectivity that individuals are folded into the state apparatus and rendered acquiescent to the status quo.

Over the last thirty years these modest anecdotes have acquired the status of premonitory parables underscoring the illusoriness of self-knowledge. Whether the work of fiction is analogous to the mirror or the police, it seeks to lull readers into a misapprehension of their existence as unified, autonomous individuals. Storytelling and the aesthetics of realism are deeply implicated in this process of misrecognition because identifying with characters is a key mechanism through which we are drawn into believing in the essential reality of persons. The role of criticism is to interrogate such fictions of selfhood; the political quiescence built into the structure of recognition must give way to a slash-and-burn interrogation of the notion of identity. Here we see the hermeneutics of suspicion cranked up to its highest level in the conviction that our everyday intuitions about persons are mystified all the way down.

That acts of misrecognition occur is not, of course, open to dispute. Who would want to deny that people deceive themselves as to their own desires or interests, that we frequently misjudge exactly who or what we are? Literary texts often serve as comprehensive compendia of such moments of fallibility, underscoring the sheer impossibility of self-transparency. Tragedy is a genre famously preoccupied with documenting the catastrophic consequences of failing to know oneself or others. And what are the novels of Austen, Eliot, or James if not testimonies to the excruciating ubiquity of misperception and false apprehension? Yet the idea of misrecognition presumes and enfolds its antithesis. In the sheer force of its judgment, it implies that a less flawed perception can be attained, that our assessments can be scrutinized and found wanting. If self-deception is hailed as the inescapable ground of subjectivity, however, it is evacuated of all critical purchase and diagnostic force, leaving us with no means of making distinctions or of gauging incremental changes in understanding. Moreover, the critic soon becomes embroiled in a version of the Cretan liar paradox. If we are barred from achieving insight or self-understanding, how could we know that an act of misrecognition had taken place? The critique of recognition, in this respect, reveals an endemic failure to face up to the normative commitments underpinning its own premises.

While recognition has received a drubbing in English departments, its fortunes have risen spectacularly in other venues. Political theorists are currently hailing recognition as a keyword of our time, a galvanizing idea that is generating new frameworks for debating the import and impact of struggles for social justice. Nancy Fraser's well-known thesis, for example, contrasts a cultural politics of recognition organized around differences of gender, race, and sexuality, to a goal of economic redistribution that defined the goals of traditional socialism. Feminism, gay and lesbian activism, and the aspirations of racial and ethnic minorities towards self-determination serve as especially visible examples of such demands for public acknowledgment. For Axel Honneth, by contrast, the search for recognition is not a new constellation driven by the demands of social movements but an anthropological constant, a defining feature of what it means to become a person that assumes multifarious cultural and political guises. Recognition, he proposes, offers a key to understanding all kinds of social inequities and struggles for self-realization, including those steered by class. What literary studies can take from these debates is their framing of recognition in terms other than gullibility. Political theory does justice to our everyday intuition that recognition is not just an error or an ensnarement, that it is, in Charles Taylor's words, a "vital human need."[6]

I need, at this point, to address a potential objection to the drift of my argument. Recognition, in the sense I've been using it so far, refers to a cognitive insight, a moment of knowing or knowing again. Specifically, I have been puzzling over what it means to say, as people not infrequently do, that I know myself better after reading a book. The ideas at play here have to do with comprehension, insight, and self-understanding. (That recognition is cognitive does not mean that it is purely cognitive, of course; moments of self-apprehension can trigger a spectrum of emotional reactions shading from delight to discomfort, from joy to chagrin.) When political theorists talk about recognition, however, they mean something else: not knowledge, but acknowledgment. Here the claim for recognition is a claim for acceptance, dignity and inclusion in public life. Its force is ethical rather than epistemic, a call for justice rather than a claim to truth. Moreover, recognition in reading revolves around a moment of personal illumination and heightened self-understanding; recognition in politics involves a demand for public acceptance and validation. The former is directed toward the self, the latter toward others, such that the two meanings of the term would seem to be entirely at odds.

Yet this distinction is far from being a dichotomy; the question of knowledge is deeply entangled in practices of acknowledgment. Stanley Cavell is fond of driving home this point in an alternate idiom: what it really means to know other people has less to do with questions of epistemological certainty than with the strength of our personal commitments. So, too, our sense of who we are is embedded in our diverse ways of being in the world and our sense of attunement or conflict with others. That this self is "socially constructed" – indisputably, we can only live our lives through the cultural resources that are available to us – does not render it any less salient: there is no meaningful sense in which we can, on a routine basis, suspend belief in our own selfhood. From such a perspective, the language game of skepticism runs up against its intrinsic limits: in Wittgenstein's well-known phrase, "doubting has an end."[7] We make little headway in grasping the ramifications of our embeddedness in the world if we remain fixated on the question of epistemic certainty or its absence.

The reasons for disciplinary disagreement on the merits of recognition are not especially hard to fathom. While political theories of recognition trace their roots back to Hegel, literary studies has been shaped by a strong strand of anti-Hegelianism in twentieth-century French thought. In this latter tradition, recognition is commonly chastised for its complicity with a logic of appropriation and a totalitarian desire for sameness. Yet such judgments conspicuously fail to do justice to its conceptual many-sidedness and suppleness, while neglecting the dialogic and non-identitarian dimensions of recognition, as anchored in intersubjective relations that precede subjectivity. The capacity for self-consciousness, for taking oneself as the object of one's own thought, is only made possible by an encounter with otherness. Recognition thus presumes difference rather than excluding it, constituting a fundamental condition for the formation of identity.[8] Insofar as selfhood arises via relation to others, self-knowledge and acknowledgment are closely intertwined. Thus theorists of intersubjectivity do not react with disappointment or distress to the news that the self is socially constituted rather than autotelic, nor do they decry such a socially created self as illusory or fictive. Rather than seeing the idea of selfhood as an epistemological error spawned by structures of ideology or discourse, they insist on the primacy of interpersonal relations in the creation of persons. We are fundamentally social creatures whose survival and well-being depend on our interactions with particular, embodied, others. The other is not a limit but a condition for selfhood.

It goes without saying that such relations between persons are filtered through the mesh of linguistic structures and cultural traditions. The I and the Thou never face each other naked and unadorned. When we speak to each other, our words are hand-me-downs, well-worn tokens used by countless others before us, the detritus of endless myths and movies, poetry anthologies and political speeches. Our language is stuffed thick with figures, larded with metaphors, encrusted with layers of meaning that escape us. While selfhood is dialogic, dialogue should not be confused with harmony, symmetry, or perfect understanding. Here we can take on board Chantal Mouffe's insistence that social relations cannot be cleansed of conflict or antagonism, and Judith Butler's claim that the Hegelian model of recognition is ultimately driven by division and self-loss.[9] Recognition is far from synonymous with reconciliation.

Yet structures that constrain also sustain; the beliefs and traditions that envelop us are a source of meaning as well as mystification. The words of the past acquire a new luster as we polish and refurbish them in our many interactions. Language is not always and only a symbol of alienation and division, but serves as a source "of mutual experiences of meaning that had been unknown before and could never have existed until fashioned by words."[10] While we never own language, we are able to borrow it and bend it to our purposes, even as aspects of what we say will continue to elude us. We are embodied and embedded beings who use and are used by words. Even as we

31

know ourselves to be shaped by language, we can reflect on our own shaping, and modify aspects of our acting and being in the world. Rather than blocking self-knowledge, language is our primary means of attaining it, however partial and flawed our attempts at understanding ourselves and others must be. We live in what Charles Taylor calls webs of interlocution; struggling to define ourselves with and against others, we acquire the capacity for reflection and self-reflection.

How do such broad-brush reflections on recognition and inter-subjectivity pertain to the specific concerns of literary studies? Literary texts invite disparate forms of recognition, serving as an ideal laboratory for probing its experiential and aesthetic complexities. Conceiving of books as persons and the act of reading as a face-to-face encounter, however, are analogies that can only lead us astray. Texts cannot think, feel, or act; if they have any impact on the world, they do so via the intercession of those who read them. And yet, while books are not subjects, they are not just objects, not simply random things stranded among countless other things. Bristling with meaning, layered with resonance, they come before us as multi-layered symbols of beliefs and values; they stand for something larger than themselves. While we do not usually mistake books for persons, we often think of them as conveying the attitudes of persons, as upholding or questioning larger ideas and collective ways of thinking.

Reading, in this sense, is akin to an encounter with a generalized other, in the phrase made famous by G. H. Mead. Like other the-orists of intersubjectivity, Mead argues that the formation of the self involves all kinds of messy entanglements, such that no "hard-and-fast line can be drawn between our own selves and the selves of others."[11] It is only by internalizing the expectations of these others that we come to acquire a sense of individuality and interior depth, or, indeed, to look askance at the very norms and values that formed us. We cannot learn the language of self-definition on our own. The idea of the generalized other is a way of describing this broader collectivity or collectivities with which we affiliate our-selves. It is not so much a real entity as an imaginary projection –

32

a conception of how others view us – that affects our actions as well as the stories we tell about ourselves. It denotes our first-person relationship to the social imaginary, the heterogeneous repertoire of stories, histories, beliefs, and ideals that frame and inform our individual histories.

Under what conditions does literature come to play a mediating role in this drama of self-formation? Often, it seems, when other forms of acknowledgment are felt to be lacking, when one feels estranged from or at odds with one's immediate milieu. Reflecting on her own passion for fiction, feminist critic Suzanne Juhasz writes: "I am lonelier in the real world situation . . . when no one seems to understand *who I am* – than by myself reading, when I feel that the book *recognizes* me, and I recognize myself because of the book."[12] Reading may offer a solace and relief not to be found elsewhere, confirming that I am not entirely alone, that there are others who think or feel like me. Through this experience of affiliation, I feel myself acknowledged; I am rescued from the fear of invisibility, from the terror of not being seen. Such moments of recognition, moreover, are not restricted to private or solitary reading; they resonate with special force when individuals come together to form a collective audience for a play or a film. Aesthetic experience crystallizes an awareness of forming part of a broader community.

A historical instance of such knowledge/acknowledgment can elucidate the theoretical point. When Ibsen's plays were first performed in England in the 1880s and 1890s, they were often staged in matinee shows catering to a largely female audience. Contemporary journalists spoke with a certain condescension of the peculiar habits of this public (its love of large hats, its habit of munching chocolate during the performance), yet they were also struck by the intensity of its involvement. Women, it seems, were prone to recognize themselves in Ibsen's work. Here is Elizabeth Robins, the well-known Ibsen actress, reacting to negative reviews of *Hedda Gabler*, a play that she was instrumental in bringing to the stage:

Mr. Clement Scott understand Hedda? – any man except that wizard Ibsen really understand her? Of course not. That was the tremendous part of it. How should men understand Hedda on the stage when they didn't understand her in the persons of their wives, their daughters, their women friends? One lady of our acquaintance, married and not noticeably unhappy, said laughing, "Hedda is all of us."[13]

What should we make of this ordinary, quite unexceptional anecdote? Among literary theorists, the usual language for explaining such sparks of affiliation is identification, a term that is, however, notoriously imprecise and elastic, blurring together distinct, even disparate, phenomena. Identification can denote a formal *alignment* with a character, as encouraged by techniques of focalization, point of view, or narrative structure, while also referencing an experiential *allegiance* with a character, as manifested in a felt sense of affinity or attachment. Critiques of identification tend to conflate these issues, assuming that readers formally aligned with a fictional persona cannot help but swallow the ideologies represented by that persona wholesale. Identification thus guarantees interpellation. In reality, the relations between such structural alignments and our intellectual or affective response are far from predictable; not only do readers vary considerably in their evaluations and attachments, but texts contain countless instances of unsympathetic protagonists or unreliable narrators whose perspective we are unlikely to take on trust.[14]

On those occasions when we experience a surge of affinity with a fictional character, moreover, the catch-all concept of identification is of little help in distinguishing between the divergent mental processes that come into play. In one possible scenario – what we might call the Madame Bovary syndrome – a reader's self-awareness is swallowed up by her intense affiliation with an imaginary persona, an affiliation that involves a temporary relinquishing of reflective and analytical consciousness. Readerly attachment takes the form of a cathexis onto idealized figures who are often treasured for their very remoteness and distance, for facilitating an escape or release from one's everyday existence. It is their very dissimilarity that is the source of their desirability. Immersed in the virtual reality of a fictional text, a reader feels herself to be transported, caught up, or swept away. I examine this condition of rapturous self-forgetting under the rubric of enchantment.

Another experience of reading, however, points back to the reader's consciousness rather than away from it, engendering a pheno-menology of self-scrutiny rather than self-loss. A fictional persona serves as a prism that refracts a revised or altered understanding of a reader's sense of who she is. The experience of self-recognition and heightened self-awareness is routed through an aesthetic medium; to see oneself as Hedda Gabler is in some sense to see one-self anew. In saying "Hedda is all of us," a woman comes to name herself differently, to look at herself in a changed light, to draw on a new vocabulary of self-description. Here an alignment with a fictional character sets into motion an interplay of self-knowledge and acknowledgment, an affiliation that is accompanied by a powerful cognitive readjustment. The idiom of identification, in other words, is poorly equipped to distinguish between the variable epistemic and experiential registers of reader involvement.[15]

A second striking aspect of the Robins quotation is its announce-ment of a plural voice, an "us" or "we." The context makes it clear that this commonality falls along the lines of gender, that the "we" being invoked is female. The claim that Hedda is "all of us" suggests that Ibsen's play speaks especially strongly to women by addressing their condition. Indeed, what the female audience recognizes in Hedda, according to Robins, is its own experience of misrecogni-tion, of not being known. Just as Ibsen's male characters have no inkling of Hedda's motives and desires; just as the male audience mem-bers fail to get Hedda and to take her part as a dramatic character; so the women in the audience are similarly misunderstood by their husbands, fathers and friends. There is a structural symmetry between text and world that brings to light a shared gender asymmetry.

Let me leave aside, for now, the merits of the claim that men can-not understand Hedda and that women inevitably do so (I will come back to this question). What is noteworthy is how this passing remark brings together the two facets of recognition I have outlined. It gives voice to a sense of illumination, a moment of self-reckoning triggered by an aesthetic encounter (Ibsen's play speaks to me, the

35

character of Hedda tells me something about my life). At the same time, it also advances an ethical and political claim for acknowledgment (Ibsen's play highlights a broader injustice, it deals with the unequal condition of women, their failure to be acknowledged as full persons). The moment of self-consciousness, of individual insight, is simultaneously a social diagnosis and an ethical judgment; a response to a work of art interfuses personal and public worlds; the desire for knowledge and the demand for acknowledgment are folded together.

To a degree that is sometimes forgotten today, Ibsen was closely identified in his lifetime with the suffragette movement and testimonies to the transformative power of his plays were fulsome and frequent. In the words of one actress: "his women are at work now in the world, interpreting women to themselves, helping to make the women of the future. He has peopled a whole new world."[16] There is no evidence that the "Hey you!" that emanated from *Hedda Gabler*, the moment of being buttonholed or interpellated by a text, lulled its audience into complacency or apathy. Ibsen's play highlights a failure of recognition, as those around Hedda seek to impose upon her familiar schemata of femininity – the radiant newly-wed, the joyful expectant mother, the femme fatale – that she protests with every pore of her being. And at least some members of its female audience recognized themselves in Hedda's plight and were brought to see the world differently.

The reception of Ibsen hardly squares with claims that realism sways its audience into acquiescence with the status quo, even as theorists who condemn its purported naïveté fail to do justice to the aesthetic self-consciousness of many realist writers. Such self-consciousness is especially apparent in the case of Ibsen, whose work repeatedly draws attention to the opacity and recalcitrance of language. Much of the action of *Hedda Gabler* takes place below the surface, in the resonance of verbal tone, gesture, and silence, in the enigmatic expressiveness of the non-said. There is a patent theatricality in the way Hedda stages her existence as a dramatic performance, an artful manipulation that leaves her underlying desires and motives obscured. "She controls herself completely," observes Lou

Andreas-Salomé, "and is an all-hardened surface, a deceptive shell, a mask prepared for every occasion."[17] With a nod to Cavell, we might describe *Hedda Gabler* as a tragedy of an unknown woman, with the proviso that Hedda wants not to be known by a man but rather to know like a man, to break free of the sheltering constraints of feminine innocence and ignorance.

It is also hard to see how realism can be accused of sustaining the fiction of autonomous selves when it embeds its characters so relentlessly in habitat and milieu. Ibsen, for example, enmeshes his characters in circumstances that shape them all the way down. Hedda's sense of alienation from her milieu, her knife-sharp irritation with the kindly fussiness of her husband and Aunt Julie, springs from an aristocratic upbringing that impels her to view her marriage as a slide into middle-class provincial drabness. Yet Ibsen also attends to the failures of interpellation, the clash of ideologies and worldviews, those instances when people turn away from the norms of selfhood held out to them, or seek to configure them differently.

What, however, should we make of the afore-mentioned claim that only women could understand Hedda while men were unable to do so? This claim will seem highly contestable, if not downright reprehensible, to several groups of critics. It cannot help but stick in the craw of those who insist on the disruptive and defamiliarizing qualities of aesthetic experience, for whom any impulse toward recognition must be strenuously resisted. Yet such a comment gives equal offense to the traditional humanist credo that great art speaks equally to everyone, by scissoring responses to Ibsen's play so emphatically along gender lines. Contemporary feminists are also likely to take issue with a gender essentialism that overlooks the fracturing of female identity by race, class, and other divisions. A passing remark thus leads us into a thicket of questions about the phenomenology of interpretation. When one recognizes oneself in a novel, a play or a film, what quality, property, or phenomenon is being recognized?

We need, first of all, to come to terms with the fact that we cannot help linking what we read, at least in part, to what we know. The current mantra of otherness insists that we can wrest ourselves free of our ingrained frameworks of reference, only to underscore the tenacious hold of such frameworks. Sara Ahmed drives home this point when she questions the possibility of an ontology of strangeness, of an encounter with pure alterity. The stranger, she observes, is always already a symbol, a marker of distinction, a freighted term within a cultural and political history that deems certain persons to be more foreign, more alien than others. As Ahmed points out, "the stranger is produced not as that which we fail to recognize, but as that which we have already recognized as 'a stranger'."[18] The point holds equally for testimonies to the otherness of literary texts; even as critics pay tribute to a work's radical singularity, they echo ingrained ideas about the ineffability and untranslatability of literature that stretch all the way back to Romanticism via Cleanth Brooks. Literary otherness is identified via a thoroughly familiar set of critical maneuvers and classifications.

This is not at all to deny that art can be a source of surprise or wonder, but to restate the rudimentary point that otherness and sameness are interfused aspects of aesthetic response, not alternate buttons one can push. Innovation and familiarity are, as Ricoeur points out, inextricably intertwined; the perception of certain phenomena as other, new, or strange depends on, and is shaped by, a prior conception of what is already known. In this regard, a notably melodramatic quality clings to the mantra of "sameness bad, difference good" echoing through much contemporary theory. "Melodramatic" tenders itself as an apposite adjective in this context, given melodrama's propensity for organizing the world in terms of Manichean moral schemes. Philosophical terms, however, do not carry their effects stamped on them in indelible ink, and the ethical and political consequences of attending to sameness or difference are far from predetermined.

If reading cannot help but involve moments of recognition, the question we face is not how to avoid such moments, but what forms they might take. In one possible scenario, recognition is triggered by a perception of direct similarity or likeness, as we encounter something that slots into a clearly identifiable scheme of things. It was by chance that I stumbled across Hilary Mantel's novel *An Experiment in Love*, only to be floored by the shock of the familiar. In Mantel's account of a Catholic girl growing up in a grimy northern English town and winning a scholarship to an elite grammar school, I found a history unnervingly close to my own. Not having lived in England for several decades, the jolt of recognition was especially intense. Mantel's book brought back memories of things long forgotten: dolly mixture; free school milk; *Judy* and *Bunty* comics; elderly women pushing shopping baskets on wheels; particular English phrases ("giving cheek"); processed peas; mothers who used to clean their children's faces by spitting on their handkerchiefs; the baroque uniforms and accouterments of English upper-class schools (Aertex blouse, gym tunic, winter skirt, school tie, blazer, shoe bag, indoor shoes, outdoor shoes . . . ).

Let me call this moment one of *self-intensification*. It is typically triggered by a skillful rendition of the densely packed minutiae of daily life: evocative smells and sounds, familiar objects and everyday things, ordinary routines, ways of talking or passing time, a reservoir of shared references from religious rituals to popular jokes to the TV shows of a certain decade. Even as we know full well that we are reading a work of fiction steered by the internal pressures of form and genre, we can be nonplussed by the clarity with which a form of life is captured. Recognizing aspects of ourselves in the description of others, seeing our perceptions and behaviors echoed in a work of fiction, we become aware of our accumulated experiences as distinctive yet far from unique. The contemporary idiom of "having an identity" owes a great deal to such flashes of intersubjective recognition, of perceived commonality and shared history. It is not especially surprising, then, that the writing and reading of fiction has often fueled the momentum of social movements.[19]

Recognition may however also take the form of what I call *self-extension*, of coming to see aspects of oneself in what seems distant or strange. When the narrator of Mishra's *The Romantics* reflects on the resonance of *Sentimental Education*, that resonance does not hinge on direct resemblance, on a commonality of cultural and historical context. Indeed, at first glance, Benares in 1989, with its crumbling buildings, bathing ghats, hordes of pilgrims, and kaleidoscope of colors, seems a world away from the nineteenth-century French capital of Flaubert's novel. With the patience of a micro-surgeon, Mishra pinpoints the endless misapprehensions, the acts of condescension and bungled gestures of friendship, that thwart the dramas of cross-cultural encounters. Californian students and the children of the French bourgeoisie seek enlightenment in India, convinced they will find a Ghandian paradise of serene, cotton-spinning, pacifist villagers. Indians dazzled by dreams of Bond Street or Rodeo Drive are convinced that the lives of Westerners are endlessly blissful and chock-full of glamor, only rarely becoming conscious of "the cruel-seeming asymmetry between desire and satisfaction that could exist in the most privileged of lives."[20]

Yet Mishra does not limit himself to documenting the disjunctures of life-worlds, to lamenting the clash and crash of alien cultures. Even as he pays tribute to *Sentimental Education* as a prototype for his own *Bildungsroman*, he uses Flaubert's novel as a leitmotif through which to explore the complex cross-hatching of likeness as well as difference. What, the narrator wonders, could a student in a provincial Indian university in the late 1980s possibly have in common with Frédéric Moreau and his generation? At first glance, the cultural, historical, and economic disparities seem glaring and all-decisive. Yet he slowly comes to realize that "the small, unnoticed tragedies of thwarted hopes and ideals Flaubert wrote about in *Sentimental Education* were all around us."[21] Not only do the narrator's unfocused longings and feelings of inadequacy mesh with those of Flaubert's hero, but modern India yields up countless stories of individuals disowning their provincial origins to seek success, only to see "their ambitions dwindle away over the years in successive disappointments."[22] What Mishra's novel suggests is that exoticizing difference, tiptoeing around other cultures by treating them as the mysterious and unknowable Other, is a perilous and deeply patronizing endeavor that blinds us to moments when histories and cultures overlap.

Shu-mei Shih has recently crafted a forceful indictment of what she calls "technologies of recognition" operative in the field of world literature, arguing that critical attention to non-Western writers is blighted by Eurocentric norms. She cites a cluster of endemic problems: sweeping generalizations and omnipotent definitions; the reduction of literary works to nationalist allegories; the marketing of multicultural identities purged of any mention of economic structures or global inequities. According to Shu-mei Shih, such practices derive from the prison house of recognition, which she parses as the reiteration of the already known, whether false presumptions of universality or Orientalist fantasies of difference. Yet her often persuasive catalogue of the various mishaps and misreadings of postcolonial studies falls short in its aim of refuting recognition, offering a notably truncated account of its doubleness and complexity. Indeed, the guiding thread of the essay, which demands that Western critics become more critical of their own practices (a call to self-knowledge) and details how non-Western literary works are often given cursory or careless treatment (a call for acknowledgment), remains entirely caught up in the premises and protocols of recognition.[23]

Mishra's allusions to *Sentimental Education*, moreover, underscore that moments of recognition are not restricted to readers addicted to the plodding veracities of realism, as its most stringent critics like to suggest. Flaubert is, of course, typically read as a proto-modernist writer under whose corrosive gaze language decomposes into an assortment of random banalities, a parroted muddle of received ideas emptied of any representational force. His work mercilessly records the various pathologies of misrecognition afflicting those who seek to glean a sense of personhood from collective fictions and counterfeit identities. The ending of *Sentimental Education* attests to the stalling of self-knowledge, as any hopes that the protagonist's worldly failures and romantic bunglings would trigger incremental gains in insight are famously frustrated. Yet the registering of such ironies also grants Flaubert's own text a diagnostic force, as an acerbic account of the failures of self-interpretation. It is in this sense that the reader's own jolt of recognition assumes a self-critical rather than consoling form; what Mishra's narrator recognizes in Frédéric Moreau, in a scenario layered with multiple levels of irony, is their shared propensity for using fictional personae as a means of self-orientation. Here acknowledgment is oriented not around a sense of shared identity, but an apprehension of a negative commonality based on a parallel history of interpretive missteps and mishaps. In calling into being a heightened self-consciousness about such mechanisms of identity formation, modernism complicates but by no means cancels a phenomenology of recognition.

One reader, for example, mentioned to me his own stab of recognition at encountering, in *To the Lighthouse*, the extended description of Mrs. Ramsay's wedge-shaped core of darkness. The tentative commonality here rests on a shared failure to be known by others (a part of oneself that remains inaccessible, that is never displayed at dinner parties or revealed to family members), yet it is a recognition that is stripped of any specific content. To assume any substantive similarity between this reader's "heart of darkness" and Mrs. Ramsay's own would be to deny her the very uniqueness and unknowability that the passage insists upon. Recognition is rendered imperfect or incomplete, in Terence Cave's terms, rather than absent.[24] While modern protagonists are less likely than their Victorian counterparts to achieve a conclusive moment of self-understanding, recognition is not so much negated as transferred to readers forced into a heightened awareness of the instabilities and opacities of personhood. Indeed, in the absence of any such mechanism it would be hard to explain the resonance of modernist texts: as Adorno points out, it is the bizarre quality of Kafka's works that renders them so uncannily familiar. Even as they block our standard strategies of interpretation and cancel out a conventional hermeneutics, they conjure up a sense of bafflement, frustration, and anxiety that many of us know all too well.

These varying models of recognition, grounded in a perception of direct likeness or metaphorical affinity, fuel much of the wrangling over literature and politics, serving as totems for warring academic tribes. The experience of reading, some critics suggest, cannot help being bound up with our desire to reflect on who and what we are; such desires are in turn tied up with differential histories, experiences of embodiment, and political realities. Our selves are sticky, in Stephen White's phrase; rather than being frictionless, disembodied and detached, they are caught up in the particulars of time and space, of culture and history, body and biography.[25] These differential circumstances matter; they demand to be acknowledged in literature as in life.

Other critics demur from what they see as an eagerness to fence readers into groups according to programmatic speculations about social identities, declaring that the value of imaginative art lies in its power to expand or extend perception. Entering other worlds, we become acquainted with the unfamiliar, are drawn to see things from different angles, glimpse aspects of ourselves in distant lives. The much decried notion of universality is simply a way of acknowledging the incontrovertible fact that literary works can resonate with readers from many different backgrounds. *Antigone* has intrigued straight men and lesbians, Norwegians and South Africans; you do not need to be an Irishman to admire James Joyce. Such an experience of extending the self, these critics conclude, trumps a sectarian aesthetics which decrees that women see themselves only in works by and about women, which would restrict gay men to a diet of Oscar Wilde, James Baldwin, and Edmund White.

Let me suggest, in response, that critics who disparage any intrusion of political affiliations into art are stricken by a failure of the very imagination that they prize so highly. If our existence pivots around the drama of recognition, our aesthetic engagement cannot be quarantined from the desire to know and to be acknowledged. We all seek in various ways to have our particularity recognized, to find echoes of ourselves in the world around us. The patent asymmetry and unevenness of structures of recognition ensure that books will often function as lifelines for those deprived of other forms of public acknowledgment. Until very recently, for example, such deprivation stamped the lives of women who desired other women; a yearning etched into the body and psyche functioned only as an absence, unmentionable at home or work, whited out in the media, invisible in public life, acknowledged only in the occasional furtive whisper or dirty joke. Reflecting on the singular impact of *The Well of Loneliness* on lesbian readers, Terry Castle speaks of its ability to engage "our deepest experience of eros, intimacy, sexual identity and how our fleshly bodies relate to the fleshly bodies of others."[26] Nor is it justifiable to shrug aside such acts of recognition as merely political rather than literary. Hall's novel resonated with readers because it fashions a narrative, not a sociological screed; because it fleshes out the drama of same-sex love through wrenching descriptions; because it draws on tragic topoi to bestow an aura of seriousness on its protagonist. Its existential and political impact is inseparable from its status as a work of fiction.

Yet it has also inspired a host of passionate repudiations: "*The Well of Loneliness*," remarks Heather Love, "still known as the most famous and most widely read of lesbian novels, is also the novel most hated by lesbians themselves."[27] Hall's tragic view of same-sex relations was to clash with subsequent conceptions of gay identity, inspiring a host of readers to disavow any conceivable parallels between themselves and Stephen Gordon. Whether or not such disavowals are justified – Love suggests that they are not – such a reception history underscores the lability and contingency of moments of recognition. Moreover, the risks of what Alexander García Düttman calls "recognition as X" (a woman/lesbian/person of color) have by now been comprehensively rehearsed.[28] To be pinned down in this way can be deeply constraining, as one's personhood is summarily defined, exhausted, and thereby reduced. The fixation on defining the self may encourage a belief that identities are governed by an immutable script, inspiring a model of repressive authenticity that leaves little room for ambiguity, disidentification, or dissent. Such convictions seem especially ill-suited to capturing what goes on in the flux of reading, when the relations between social demographics and particular patterns of affiliation and recognition are often fluid and unpredictable. Matching up the identities of readers and characters, assuming that recognition requires direct resemblance, means, in essence, denying the metaphorical and self-reflexive dimensions of literary representation.

Let me return one last time to *Hedda Gabler*. At the time of its first performance, the impact of Ibsen's play lay in the ruthlessness with which it ripped off the mask of domestic harmony, exposing the chasm that yawned between men and women. One of the first plays to center on a heroine's sense of panicked entrapment, to zero in on a woman's revulsion with the roles of wife and mother, it opened up new and disturbing lines of thought. What exactly is woman's nature? Do all women share the same nature? How exactly does one justify the denial of male freedoms to women? The confrontational nature of such questions should not be underestimated. At a time when suffragettes were still often dismissed as a lunatic fringe, Ibsen's plays brought issues of female emancipation into the middle-class drawing room. Rather than addressing everyone equally, they opened up painful and politically charged schisms in their audience. The historical record suggests that women and men were often divided over the merits of *Hedda Gabler* and that Ibsen's play made some women more aware – or differently aware – of their status as women.

Yet nowadays, the meaning of Ibsen's play no longer seems quite so firmly fixed by the gender divide. A substantial body of work by critics and directors has put paid to the claim that men are inherently incapable of understanding Hedda. What she symbolizes for women may also have changed. In the last three decades we have heard countless stories about frustrated women trapped in loveless marriages: what seems revelatory now is not so much Ibsen's exposure of the hidden dramas of domestic discontent as his audacious conception of his heroine. I came of age at a time when feminism was associated with claims about women's essential difference from men, amplified by copious references to female nurturing, an ethics of care, and the moral superiority of women. Ibsen gives us the antithesis of such a woman-identified woman, a protagonist who is arrogant, callous, and openly self-centered, who flinches away from any association with the feminine. What now seems remarkable is the boldness with which Ibsen severs morality from politics, suggesting that women's likeability or goodness has nothing to do with the legitimacy of their demand for freedom. Rather than being synonymous with feminism, Ibsen's heroine now offers a prescient commentary on feminist tendencies to idealize and circumscribe what it meant to be a woman. The recognition triggered by *Hedda Gabler* rather than confirming the clarity of the gender divide, frays and unravels its already tattered edges.

Literary texts thus offer an exceptionally rich field for parsing the complexities of recognition. Through their attentiveness to particulars, they possess the power to promote a heightened awareness of the density and distinctiveness of particular life-worlds, of the stickiness of selves. And yet they also spark elective affinities and imaginative affiliations that bridge differences and exceed the literalism of demographic description. Such texts, moreover, can also underscore the limits of knowability through structures of negative recognition that underscore the opacity of persons and their failure to be fully transparent to themselves or others. Rather than simply debunking or disrupting recognition, in other words, the literary field offers endless illustrations of its complexity as an experiential mode and an analytical concept. As my examples show, recognition does not require or revolve around an immutable kernel of literary content. We do not glimpse aspects of ourselves in literary works because these works are repositories for unchanging truths about the human condition, as conservative critics like to suggest. Rather, any flash of recognition arises from an interplay between texts and the fluctuating beliefs, hopes, and fears of readers, such that the insights gleaned from literary works will vary dramatically across space and time.

In this regard, the condition of intersubjectivity precludes any programmatic ascription of essential traits to oneself or others. If selfhood is formed in a dialogic and relational fashion, no basis exists for ascribing an unchanging core of identity to one or more members of a group. What it means to be a certain kind of person will shift in accordance with external forces, under the pressure of seismological shifts in attitudes and forms of life. None of us have unmediated access to our own selves, which we are called on to interpret through the cultural resources available to us. R. Radhakrishnan rightly insists that recognition's entanglement with structures of linguistic and cultural representation precludes the possibility of authentic or primordial being.[29] Yet the flattening out of subjectivity in current theory, the off-hand references to persons as bundles of signifiers or textual effects, engenders a singularly flimsy and unsatisfying model of the self that is unable to explain either the phenomenon of self-consciousness – our ability to reflect on, and in some cases to modify, what we are – or why particular

46

representations may strike a chord with some groups and not with others. Virtually every aspect of our behavior and interaction reveals a complex interplay of individualized predispositions, deep cultural influences, and reflexive practices of self-interpretation and adjustment that is poorly captured by the often anodyne rhetoric of social construction.

Having brought together knowledge and acknowledgment, I want in conclusion to prise them apart, to highlight the potential tensions and frictions between the dynamics of literary recognition and the desire for public affirmation. When political theorists speak of the politics of recognition, they are referring not only to a public acknowledgment of someone's existence, but also to an affirmation of its value. Reacting against a history of condescension and marginalization, women and minorities seek to affirm their distinctiveness and to have it affirmed by others. To be recognized, in this sense, does not just mean having one's differences noticed (for they were always noticed), but having those differences seen as desirable and worthy. Steven Rockefeller, for example, claims that "the call for recognition of the value of different cultures is the expression of a basic and profound universal human need for unconditional acceptance." Writing in a more openly psychoanalytical vein, Suzanne Juhasz argues that the recognition that women find in books is a form of affirmation akin to the nurturing and empathy of maternal love.[30] In these and similar observations, stress is laid on the positive value to be assigned to particular persons or groups of persons.

Such a vision of recognition as unconditional affirmation collides with any notion of recognition as clarifying self-scrutiny, given that the latter process is likely to be discomfiting, even unpleasant, requiring a reckoning with one's own less appealing motivations and desires. Here literary studies offers a further adjustment and amplification to political debates over recognition. Over the years, literary and cultural critics have sporadically called for positive images of disenfranchised groups, yet such attempts tend to attract little support and soon run out of steam, in large part because of their awkward proximity to aesthetic idealism: the pre-modern doctrine that art should uplift its audience by depicting virtuous and unblemished

47

persons. In modernity, however, we are often drawn to literary texts for quite other reasons, including their willingness to catalogue the extent of our duplicities, deceptions, and destructive desires. While the language of positive images is an understandable reaction to a historical archive of malicious or salacious representations, it enacts its own form of symbolic violence in erasing the complexity and many-sidedness of persons and censoring contradictory impulses or inadmissible yearnings.

The Lacanian picture of the child gazing entranced at its own idealized self-image thus falls notably short as a schema for capturing how literature represents selves. The experience of reading is often akin to seeing an unattractive, scowling, middle-aged person coming into a restaurant, only to suddenly realize that you have been looking into a mirror behind the counter and that this unappealing-looking person is you. Mirrors do not always flatter; they can take us off our guard, pull us up short, reflect our image in unexpected ways and from unfamiliar angles. Many of the works we call tragic, for example, relentlessly pound home the refractoriness of human subjectivity, the often disastrous gap between intentions and outcomes, the ways in which persons commonly misjudge themselves and others. We can value literary works precisely because they force us – in often unforgiving ways – to confront our failings and blind spots rather than shoring up our self-esteem.

Literary texts offer us new ways of seeing, moments of heightened self-apprehension, alternate ways of what Proust calls reading the self. Knowing again can be a means of knowing afresh, and recognition is far from synonymous with repetition, complacency, and the dead weight of the familiar. Such moments of heightened insight are not just personal revelations in a private communion between reader and text; they are also embedded in circuits of acknowledgment and affiliation between selves and others that draw on and cut across the demographics of social life. While the language of identification has triggered much unproductive wrangling over the precise value of identity, recognition does not depend on the integrity of self-identity in the same way. Because it is anchored in a dialogic relation rather than a core personhood, the question of what we recognize in texts or persons can receive many different answers. I would dispute Patchen Markell's claim that theorists of recognition assume the possibility of a world of mutual transparency, a world without alienation, where identity is treated as a fait accompli.[31] This strikes me as an inaccurate, even unjust, characterization of the work of Nancy Fraser, Axel Honneth, or Charles Taylor, all of whom conceive of recognition as a far more ambiguous, conflictual, and open-ended process than such a statement suggests.

In a well-known essay, Foucault warns against any attempt to find moments of continuity and resemblance in history, speaking dismissively of the "consoling play of recognitions."[32] Against such all too frequent polemical jabs, I have argued that the phenomenology of recognition brings into play the familiar and the strange, the old and the new, the self and the non-self. It may help to confirm and intensify a sense of particularity, but it may also cut across and confuse familiar rubrics of identity. Recognition is about knowing, but also about the limits of knowing and knowability, and about how self-perception is mediated by the other, and the perception of otherness by the self. Precisely because of its fundamental doubleness, its oscillation between knowledge and acknowledgment, the epistemological and the ethical, the subjective and the social, the phenomenology of recognition calls for more attention in literary and cultural studies.

"What guarantees the security and authority of the cognitive 'categories' of the knowing subject?" asks Christopher Prendergast in an argument that voices qualified sympathy for the idea of recognition. Yet the question is surely misplaced, voicing an impossible demand for guarantees that threatens to plunge us back into skepticism's treacherous waters. Any pursuit of self-knowledge is dogged by difficulty and the shadow of failure, tied to all the usual epistemic risks of error, blindness, and confusion.[33] The insights we glean from reading are precarious if no less precious, fallible, and imperfect, flashes of illumination flanked by shadowy zones of unknowingness. What once seemed like an epiphany may continue to resonate and transform our lives, or it may turn out to be less momentous than we once thought. The narrator of *The Romantics* find his self-understanding permanently enriched and deepened by the tangled layers of affinity he uncovers between himself and Frédéric Moreau. By contrast, Thomas Buddenbrooks soon forgets the insights he gleaned from the pages of Schopenhauer and dies ignominiously from a stroke not long after, even as the novel withholds any final judgment as to the truth of the philosopher's words. Recognition comes without guarantees; it takes place in the messy and mundane world of human action, not divine revelation. Yet it remains, in its many guises – including the rueful recognition of the limits of recognition – an indispensable means of making sense of texts and of the world.

# 2

# *Enchantment*

The US critic and queer theorist Joseph Boone launches his book on modernism and sexuality with an impassioned defense of close reading. Writing at a time when cultural studies is on the ascendant, Boone feels the need to defend his desire to linger over the textures and rhythms of words, to take apart and piece together novelistic plots, to spin out intricate webs of textual analysis. Enlisting the support of Eve Sedgwick, he argues that close reading, far from being a dry-as-dust exercise in dissecting sentences, entails an ardent involvement with what he calls the numinous power of aesthetic objects. He speaks of "threading one's way through the mazes of plot and counterplot in those long, lovely novelistic fictions whose enticements, mysteries, and eventual rewards encourage that willing suspension of disbelief, that delirious process of surrender into otherness."[1] For Boone, close reading is about intoxication rather than detachment, rapture rather than disinterestedness. It is, above all, about learning to surrender, to give oneself up, a yielding that is not abject or humiliating, but ecstatic and erotically charged. Through the act of reading, he writes, we can experience a condition of "absolute *powerlessness*, enacting the intense human desire to let go – to be released, to yield to an 'other'."[2]

The wide-eyed face of Mia Farrow dominates the opening and closing scenes of *The Purple Rose of Cairo*, as she gazes up at the movie screen in a state of utter absorption. Farrow plays the role of a young woman mired in poverty and an unhappy marriage in the dog days of the Depression. The movie theater serves as her solace and refuge, allowing her to banish, if only briefly, the aggravations and afflictions of the work-a-day world. The glossy black-and-white aesthetic of her favorite film, "The Purple Rose of Cairo," with its glamorous adventurers, endless dry martinis, and dinners at the Copacabana, offers a stark visual counterfoil to the dun-colored drabness of her workplace and her marriage. Farrow's character loses herself in a way that we are often encouraged to think of as escapist and mindless, yet her beatific expression, as her radiant face fills up the screen, announces a state of pure bliss that is not so easily discounted. When dashing explorer Tom Baxter steps down off the screen and comes striding toward her, she is not especially nonplussed, for the world of the film has become more vividly present to her than her own.

The scrupulous attentiveness to stylistic and narrative detail invoked by Boone is often seen as the hallmark of criticism, as what people have in mind when they hold forth on the merits of reading literature "as literature." The practice of close reading is tacitly viewed by many literary scholars as the mark of their tribe – as what sets them apart, in the last instance, from their like-minded colleagues in sociology or history. It persists in published criticism, remains a staple in the classroom, has weathered the onslaught of endless theories, crops up in new work on feeling and affect, Deleuze and disability studies. Academic fashions may come and go, but a sharply honed attentiveness to nuances of language and form is still held, by most scholars and teachers of literature, as an indispensable sign of competence in their field. It simply is, in Rorty's phrase, what we do around here.

Being enthralled by a film, by contrast, is associated with more homespun and vernacular forms of aesthetic response driven by the dream worlds of mass culture. Popular art is often accused of disorienting and bewitching its audience, calling up an association of art with magic that stretches back to antiquity. For much of the *longue durée* of modernity, the novel is the genre most frequently accused of casting a spell on its readers; like a dangerous drug, it lures them away from their everyday lives in search of heightened sensations and undiluted pleasures. Disoriented by the power of words, readers are no longer able to distinguish between reality and imagination; deprived of their reason, they act like mad persons and fools. *Don Quixote* inaugurates a swathe of novels anxious to diagnose the dangers of such mind-altering fictions while advertising themselves as their cure. Modernism, especially, announces itself as an art of disenchantment, initiating copious commentary on literature's counterfeit status and its power to beguile and deceive. Meanwhile, film will soon supplant the novel as the medium most often accused of lulling its viewers into a trance-like fascination with unreal worlds.

Women are often seen as especially prone to such acts of covert manipulation. Susceptible and suggestible, lacking intellectual distance and mastery over their emotions, they are all too easily swept up in a world of intoxicating illusions. Aesthetic enchantment leads inexorably to ontological confusion, to a disturbing failure to differentiate between fact and fantasy, reality and wish fulfillment. In his description of Emma Bovary's visit to the opera and her reaction to *Lucia di Lammermoor*, Flaubert invites us to observe a case study in such feminine absorption. Caught up in a tumult of feeling, Emma sees her own destiny echoed and magnified in the prima donna's agonized lamentations. All pretense of aesthetic distance is wiped out as the encounter with Donizetti's opera triggers an ecstatic yielding and melting, a form of quasi-lascivious abandonment. The erotic undertow of aesthetic enchantment becomes all too evident as Emma, caught up in a mélange of chaotic and swirling emotions, mistakes the male singer for his role. "A mad idea took possession of her: he was looking at her right now! She longed to run to his arms, to take refuge in his strength, as in the incarnation of love itself, and to say to him, to cry out, 'Take me away! carry me with you! let us leave! All my passion and all my dreams are yours!' "[3]

The two vignettes of aesthetic response with which this chapter opens – the literary critic parsing the prose of James Joyce and Virginia Woolf, the working-class woman enthralled by a Hollywood movie – seem at first glance to be worlds apart. One form of attention is micro, paying fastidious attention to the luminous aesthetic detail; the other is macro, involving an all-embracing sense of being swept up into another world. The first requires a literary education in the protocols of close reading; the second epitomizes the seductive pull of popular entertainment. From a certain standpoint – the standpoint of Pierre Bourdieu, let us say – these images could well serve as a clinching testimony of the class-based stratification of aesthetic experience. Yet they are also tied together by a common experience of enchantment, of total absorption in a text, of intense and enigmatic pleasure. The experience of being wrapped up in a novel or a film – whether "high" or "low"– confounds our deeply held beliefs about the rationality and autonomy of persons.

Enchantment is a term with precious little currency in literary theory, calling up scenarios of old-school professors swooning in rapture over the delights of Romantic poetry. Contemporary critics pride themselves on their power to disenchant, to mercilessly direct laser-sharp beams of critique at every imaginable object. In Lyotard's words, "demystification is an endless task."[4] Yet this desire to purge aesthetic experience of its enigmatic and irrational qualities merely has the effect of driving them underground. While critics do not talk of enchantment, it does not follow that they have never been enchanted. What follows is an attempt to find surer footing for a condition of aesthetic absorption that is frequently portrayed in literature and film but rarely awarded sustained or sympathetic attention in theory.

Enchantment is characterized by a state of intense involvement, a sense of being so entirely caught up in an aesthetic object that nothing else seems to matter. Stephen Greenblatt writes, "looking may be called enchanted when the act of attention draws a circle around itself from which everything but the object is excluded."[5] Wrapped up in the details of a novel, a film, a painting, you feel yourself enclosed in a bubble of absorbed attention that is utterly distinct from the hit-and-miss qualities of everyday perception. This sense of immersion seems self-enclosed and self-sustaining, demarcated by a distinct boundary; the transition back to the everyday world feels unwelcome, even intrusive. As the credits roll and the house lights come back on, as you reluctantly close the pages of the book and look up at the world around you, there is an awkward moment of readjustment, a shuddering change of gear, a momentary twinge of sorrow or regret.

Enchantment is soaked through with an unusual intensity of perception and affect; it is often compared to the condition of being intoxicated, drugged, or dreaming. Colors seem brighter, perceptions are heightened, details stand out with a hallucinatory sharpness. The effect can be uniquely exhilarating, because of the sheer intensity of the pleasure being offered, but also unnerving, in sapping a sense of autonomy and self-control. The analytical part of your mind recedes into the background; your inner censor and critic are nowhere to be found. Instead of examining a text with a sober and clinical eye, you are pulled irresistibly into its orbit. There is no longer a sharp line between self and text but a confused and inchoate intermingling. Possessing some of the viscerality of shock, enchantment has none of its agitating and confrontational character; it offers rapturous self-forgetting rather than self-shattering. You feel oblivious to your surroundings, your past, your everyday life; you exist only in the present and the numinous presence of a text.

Not only your autonomy but your sense of agency is under siege. You have little control over your response; you turn the pages compulsively, you gaze fixedly at the screen like a sleepwalker. Descriptions of enchantment often pinpoint an arresting of motion, a sense of being transfixed, spellbound, unable to move, even as your mind is transported elsewhere. Time slows to a halt: you feel yourself caught in an eternal, unchanging present. Rather than having a sense of mastery over a text, you are at its mercy. You are sucked in, swept up, spirited away, you feel yourself enfolded in a blissful embrace. You are mesmerized, hypnotized, possessed. You strain to reassert yourself, but finally you give in, you stop struggling, you yield without a murmur.

Is it at all surprising that aesthetic enchantment has received a bad press among politically minded critics? Brecht's well-known outburst of irritation sets the tone:

> We can hardly accept the theatre as we see it before us. Let us go into one of these houses and observe the effect which it has on the

spectators. Looking about us, we see somewhat motionless figures in a peculiar condition: they seem strenuously to be tensing all their muscles, except where these are flabby and exhausted. They scarcely communicate with each other; their relations are those of a lot of sleepers . . . True, their eyes are open, but they stare rather than see, just as they listen rather than hear. They look at the stage as if in a trance, an expression which comes from the Middle Ages, the days of witches and priests.[6]

As Brecht would have it, the theater audience is an anachronism, a sorry hold-over from a time of superstition and primitive belief. In its dazed, dream-like state, it calls to mind a long-gone era of demonic possession and magic ritual. Such reactions can only be a jarring anomaly in a scientific age that prides itself on skepticism and rational inquiry. Reason does not exclude pleasure, but it delivers, according to Brecht, a different kind of pleasure, intermingled with reflection and judgment. The epic theater will cultivate a critical perspective in its audience, allowing them to lean back thoughtfully and to assess what is happening on the stage rather than surrendering to a hypnotic trance.

Like Brecht, many literary scholars have prided themselves on their power to demystify and their vigilant stance. We need only think of a history of feminist critiques of visual pleasure and the male gaze, Marxist analyses of aesthetic ideology and commodity fetishism, the poststructuralist idiom of suspicion and interrogation, New Historicist indictments of power and containment. Critics seek to go behind the scenes, to expose the clay feet of idols or to smash them to pieces, to prove that beautiful images serve as a screen for perfidious political realities. Enchantment, in this sense, is the antithesis and enemy of criticism. To be enchanted is to be rendered impervious to critical thought, to lose one's head and one's wits, to be seduced by what one sees rather than subjecting it to sober and level-headed scrutiny.

There are countless difficulties tied up with enchantment. The word implies there is something elusive about aesthetic experience, an ineffable and enigmatic quality that resists rational analysis. Depending on one's perspective, such a claim can come across as anti-intellectual, half-baked, even proto-fascist. Enchantment's suggestion of occultism and sorcery skirts dangerously close to the edges of secular thought; the very idea of magic clashes with the fundamental tenets of modernity, invoking a world that has been relegated to the scrutiny of anthropologists and historians. If critics leave any room for the experience of enchantment, they are inclined to diagnose it as a displacement of real-world issues, a symptom of something else. Theories of commodity fetishism, for example, find magic in modernity only to explain it away as a form of mystification steered by the logic of the capitalist system. Enchantment is bad magic, and the role of criticism is to break its spell by providing rational explanations for seemingly irrational phenomena.

The default position of contemporary criticism is best described as one of "standing back" – keeping one's distance from a work of art in order to place it in an explanatory frame, whether drawn from politics, psychoanalysis, or philosophy. The protocols of academic skepticism urge us to view every possible phenomenon as a product of contingent and changeable circumstances. (Conversely, to take things for granted, to see them as natural or inevitable, is the most heinous of sins.) From such a perspective, enchantment is an alarming prospect. If we are entirely caught up in a text, we can no longer place it in a context because it *is* the context, imperiously dictating the terms of its reception. We are held in a condition of absorption, in Michael Fried's terms, transfixed and immobilized by the work and rendered unable to frame, contextualize, or judge.[7] The idea of enchantment implies that a mysterious something emanates from a work and subliminally steers the reader's or viewer's response. We are the objects of sorcery, not its subjects.

Here as elsewhere, arguments about art turn out to rely on tacit beliefs about the nature of social reality that deserve closer scrutiny. Max Weber's thesis about the disenchantment of the world remains an essential touchstone. Weber famously claimed that scientific progress has leached the world of any sense of the sacred, of ultimate meaning. "There are no mysterious incalculable forces that come into play . . . one can, in principle, master all things by calculation.

57

This means that the world is disenchanted. One need no longer have recourse to magical means in order to master or implore the spirits, as did the savage, for whom such mysterious powers existed. Technical means and calculations perform the service."[8] In modern societies, the mysteries of magical ritual have yielded to the rule of the calculator and the computer. Yet technical problem-solving, while giving us the ability to design ever more complicated cell-phones, is unable to bestow purpose on our lives or on our deaths. Now that the gods are destroyed, we are spiritually bereft, unable to find answers to the question most important to us: "What shall we do and how shall we live?"

Long taken as an article of faith by social theorists, Weber's thesis is now being challenged from various directions. Is modernity really synonymous with rationalization? Is enchantment entirely absent from the world? In *The Enchantment of Modern Life*, Jane Bennett assails Weber's ideas, proposing an alternative view of modernity as awash with wonder, surprise, affective attachments. The end of divine purpose does not mean an end to enchantment, which she defines in secular rather than sacred terms as a sensuous and joyful immersion in the marvelous specificity of things. Finding the experience of wonder in animal hybrids and scientific photographs, in the work of Kafka as well as Gap commercials, Bennett urges us to cultivate and cherish experiences of enchantment, to wean ourselves from an endemic mindset of pessimism and critique. An affirmation of wonder is potentially enlivening, energizing, even ethical, encouraging a stance of openness and generosity to the world. Conversely, the discourse of disenchantment reiterates and reinforces the very condition that it describes, sinking us ever deeper into the void of a dispiriting, self-corroding skepticism.[9]

Such an argument strikes at the heart of modernity's self-image, calling on us to reassess a history of thought that defines modernity against the hidebound superstitions of tradition and that can only conceive of the irrational as an atavistic residue. It asks us to open our eyes to the enduring enchantments of modernity, to acknowledge the persistence of the marvelous in the present. Here Bennett joins a cohort of thinkers who are questioning the purported ubiquity

and irreversibility of disenchantment. Postcolonial scholars, in particular, have mounted vigorous critiques of the modern tendency to
counterpose rationality against religion, secularism against superstition. Rather than initiating a decisive break with hide-bound beliefs
and anachronistic attachments, they argue, modernity in its multiple
forms, from New York to New Delhi, remains deeply entangled with
magical and mythical thought.[10]

Yet Bennett's distance from Weber is not quite as great as she thinks.
If we look carefully at "Science as a Vocation," we find that Weber
is far from equating modernity with the triumph of arid calculation
and Gradgrindian rationality. Indeed, he makes a point of arguing
that scientific progress is driven by the magic of inspired ideas rather
than plodding calculation. Such ideas have their own mysterious and
unfathomable rhythms, descending when least expected or refusing
to appear at all. For Weber, science is in many respects analogous
to art: success in both fields is driven by unpredictable surges of creativity, inspiration, frenzy, mania. Indeed, he deliberately disenchants
the idea of disenchantment by pointing out that "only a hair line
separates faith from science."[11] While Weber sees the world as rationalized in the sense of being robbed of transcendental meaning, he
is far from claiming that our engagement with that world is ruled
by the iron law of logic. Modernity may exclude the supernatural,
yet it remains saturated with the superrational. While the world is
no longer enchanted, in other words, we are still prone to experiences of enchantment.

Literary theory, however, rushed in to complete the task that Weber
left unfinished, driven by a nervousness about literature's awkward
proximity to imagination, emotion, and other soft, fuzzy, ideas.
Structuralism, with its armory of semiotic and quasi-scientific
terminology, sought to void aesthetic experience of any residue of
ambiguity, idiosyncrasy, or surprise. The self was demoted to a mere
nodal point through which the anonymous codes of culture buzzed
and hummed, with entirely foreseeable results. And while deconstruction brought back a sense of the aleatory and indeterminate into
interpretation, its deep-rooted suspicion of metaphysical presences and
myths of origins – its stance of what Rorty calls "knowingness" –

was equally distrustful of the idea of enchantment. Deconstructive critics chafing against the tradition of the Enlightenment often seemed unaware that their own intensely honed skepticism was derived from that same tradition. Perhaps the closest theoretical analogue to enchantment was *jouissance*, that quintessentially eighties word once reverentially traded back and forth in graduate seminars. Yet, however enigmatic and inexplicable it was often claimed to be, *jouissance* did not include the experience of munching popcorn while being engrossed in the latest episode of *Star Wars*. It was a forbidding, highbrow, Parisian kind of pleasure, a transgressive frisson inspired by the Marquis de Sade, not chanteuse Sade.

If enchantment is often associated with popular fiction and film, we might expect cultural studies to yield fresh insights. Yet cultural critics have been hell-bent on disproving the view that consumers of popular art are enchanted, hailing them as savvy interpreters, knowing negotiators, deftly wending their way between competing meanings and frameworks. For cultural studies, it is a sacred tenet that the popular consumer is an alert and critical consumer. Such acts of redescription were fueled by intense irritation with standard intellectual accounts of a stupefied, slack-jawed mass audience held captive by the opiates of rap music and reality TV. Only a certain kind of Cambridge don or Californian Marxist could really believe that viewers without advanced degrees lack all irony, skepticism, or critical distance when faced with the more vacuous offerings of the film and television industry. And yet, this emphasis on the knowing agency of audiences has also occluded the perplexing elements of aesthetic experience that come into view when we speak of being swept up, transported, taken out of ourselves. Such elements, I am suggesting, may cut across the distinction between high and low art rather than reinforcing it.

Indeed, J. Hillis Miller has recently ventured to describe literature as a form of secular magic.[12] In his latest book the arch-exponent of deconstruction revisits the scenes of his childhood in order to reflect on his early experiences of being carried away by a book. This primordial enchantment continues to shape his later engagement as a reader, even as it has remained underground, unacknowledged until now by the adult critic. A literary work, writes Miller, works like an abracadabra or hocus pocus that open up an unfamiliar world; its opening words transport us, as if through sorcery, into an alternative universe. He writes of being enraptured by what he reads, pulled into a strange hallucinatory state of consciousness more akin to dreaming than waking.

Miller's language here is remarkably similar to that of a quite different reader, Richard Hillyer, a self-educated cowman's son, describing his youthful discovery of Tennyson and other well-known writers at the dawn of the twentieth century:

> The coloured words flashed out and entranced my fancy. They drew pictures in the mind. Words become magical, incantations, abracadabra which called up spirits ... Here in books was a limitless world that I could have for my own. It was like coming up from the bottom of the ocean and seeing the world for the first time.[13]

Standard histories of reading and working-class education, directing their energies towards an expose of their disciplinary and regulative powers, have all but ignored the ways in which access to books could be subjectively experienced in a very different register, as an introduction to a shimmering, magical, world full of strange, fantastical scenarios and undreamed-of possibilities.

Miller also underscores the affinities between literature and modern media as alternative forms of virtual reality. Rather than being at odds with modernity, magic lies at its very heart, its powers of enchantment extended and accentuated by the inventiveness of new technologies. In the phrase popularized by that Ur-text of cyberpunk, *Neuromancer*, we could think of literature as a longstanding and especially successful form of consensual hallucination. Miller's *On Literature* seeks to make sense of the vivid presence of the fictional world conjured up by words, the ways in which what does not exist comes to seem vividly, achingly real. How is it that black squiggles on a page can conjure up such vivid simulacra of persons, things, actions, places; that readers can experience such powerful sensations and emotions as we react to these shadows and phantasms?

Literature seems akin to sorcery in its power to turn absence into presence, to summon up spectral figures out of the void, to conjure images of hallucinatory intensity and vividness, to fashion entire worlds into which the reader is swallowed up.

Here, Hillis Miller joins forces with other critics seeking to develop a lexicon more attuned to the affective and absorbing aspects of reading. Less invested in the archetype of the detached and dispassionate critic, feminist critics have often been more willing to admit to, and to elucidate, their intense involvement in literary texts. Lynn Pearce, for example, describes an emotional disturbance, a rich chaos and confusion at the heart of her own history of reading, that standard theoretical idioms leave her poorly equipped to address. And in an engaging series of autobiographical reflections, Janice Radway contrasts her New Critical training in a carefully qualified rhetoric of irony and ambiguity with her own memories of a passionate, quasi-visceral engagement with works of fiction. She speaks of a narrative hypnosis, an intense involvement of both mind and body in the act of reading, a peculiar act of transubstantiation, "whereby 'I' become something other than what I have been and inhabit thoughts other than those I have been able to conceive before."[14]

Such an experience of self-surrender is often associated with genres that cater to escapist yearnings and that proffer their readers or viewers the narcissistic bliss of idealized self-images. In *Don Quixote* and *Madame Bovary* it is the dream worlds of romance that delight and delude the minds of the protagonists, as judged by the seemingly more scrupulous and hard-headed perspective of the narrative frame. Romance in its various guises undoubtedly feeds a craving to be totally loved or unconditionally admired, proffering a momentary release from the reign of the mediocre and mundane, from the endless drudgery of daily compromise and concession. And yet readers testify to being entranced by a motley array of genres and forms, from lyric poetry to realist novels to postmodern fiction. Moreover, while critics often assume that absorption is tied to the experience of identifying with fictional characters, the catalysts for such involvement turn out to be less predictable.

In an interesting discussion of the phenomenology of immersion, Marie-Laure Ryan suggests that language itself seems to fade away. Readers are so entirely caught up in what they are reading that the verbal medium is effaced: they no longer perceive or register the words they are scanning, but feel themselves to be fully subsumed with an imagined world.[15] While Ryan captures well the quality of one kind of aesthetic enchantment, she fails to consider the possibility of being seduced by a style, assuming that any attention to language will be purely cerebral and analytical in nature. What such an argument overlooks is the possibility of an emotional, even erotic cathexis onto the sounds and surfaces of words. Here language is not a hurdle to be vaulted over in the pursuit of pleasure, but the essential means to achieving it. We need only think of those moments when a reader, on opening a book, is drawn in by a cadence of tone, by particular inflections and verbal rhythms, by an irresistible combination of word choice and syntax. In her reflections on how queerness can inspire passionate attachments to particular texts, Eve Sedgwick speaks of "a visceral near-identification with the writing I cared for, at the level of sentence structure, metrical pattern, rhyme."[16] Fluctuating intensities of affinity and involvement are conjured out of the bare bones of intonation and modulation, ways of speaking, timbre and tonality, the tempo of style.

Readers prone to such infatuations, we might assume, are likely to be drawn to idiosyncratic, edgy, even flamboyant examples of language use. Yet among those writers who attract the most intense scrutiny and capacious commentary are authors frequently deemed to have no style at all, or rather, to have achieved the ideal of a styleless style scoured clean of any blemish of particularity. Critics who explicate the details of point of view or pore over the technicalities of indirect style libre remain silent on the question of why the impersonal detachment of certain writers – Flaubert, for example – inspires such personal attachment on their own part, causing them to devote much of their lives to its painstaking, even obsessive, analysis.

D. A. Miller touches on such issues in his recent meditations on Austen and style. He dwells on the siren lure of Jane Austen's voice, an enchantment that he attributes to a singularly impersonal beauty of expression. Such god-like detachment, he suggests, finds few peers in the English realist novel, whose narrators are more likely to drop into the recognizable roles of bluff jovial uncles or solicitous mothers. What we encounter in Austen, by contrast, is not stylishness, but Style itself, a supremely disembodied narrative stance emptied of all markers of the person, its features most commonly evoked through metaphors of jewelry – crystalline, sparkling, dazzling, glittering, gem-like – or cutting – sharp, keen, incisive. Miller juxtaposes Austenian style as a feature of narration to style as an element of character; while a heroine's feisty words and sparkling wit serve to attract the hero's attention while warding off the dolts and dullards, such style exists to be relinquished at the moment when she faces up to her own desire to be married. At the heart of Austen style, in other words, is a vexed relationship to the conjugal imperative; the sharp edges and flashing surfaces of Austen's own narrative stance, if wholeheartedly embraced by her female characters, would permanently stall the machinery of the marriage plot in which these characters are enmeshed.

Miller begins his essay by invoking the primal shame of the boy who is caught reading Jane Austen. For such a boy, the lure of Austen's style – what Miller calls its thrilling inhumanness – may offer a temporary severance from a personhood that is felt to be anomalous, queer, out of place. Such a reader, Miller suggests, is analogous to Austen herself, who wields style to conceal the stigma of her own spinsterhood, a condition that could never be affirmed in her own work. Style, in this quintessentially Barthesian sense, is hailed as an emptying out of the self, a fugitive release from the pains of a damaged identity. And yet, the boy's devotion to Austen also marks him as patently at odds with the norms of his gender – especially, one suspects, in the contemporary US. While style, through its fastidious attention to the selecting and shaping of signifiers, seeks to deflect attention away from a depth model of the self, it also bears the indelible stain of a lacking or failed masculinity. The homosexual, remarks Miller, has come to serve as a lightning rod for a culture wary of the "extreme, exclusive, emptying, ecstatic, character of *any* serious experience of Style."[17]

In one of his footnotes, Miller frames his reading of Austen as an implicit polemic against forms of historicism that remain scandalously indifferent to the originality of her literary achievement. Analogous complaints are being hurled at literary studies from a variety of directions; we hear ever more frequently that ideology critique has triumphed at the expense of aesthetics, that pleasing surfaces have been entirely subsumed by programmatic political judgments, that critics have lost sight of the distinctive visual qualities and verbal textures of works of art. The much heralded return to beauty is one attempt to reorient the critical conversation; beauty bespeaks a positive value, a presence, an enrichment, even if the precise nature of that enrichment often eludes our analytical grasp. The new writing on beauty thus overlaps at key points with the phenomenology of enchantment. And yet much of this new work rehearses some very old prejudices against commercial and mass-mediated art in its conviction that only an encounter with Matisse or Mozart can trigger rapture, wonder, or self-loss.[18]

*Spirited Away*, one of a dazzling and highly successful sequence of anime directed by Hayao Miyazaki, recounts the adventures of a young protagonist, Chihiro, after she and her parents wander into what appears to be an abandoned theme park. After they gorge themselves on the tempting delicacies displayed at a food stall, her mother and father are transformed into grunting pigs. As she flees in horror, Chihiro finds her escape cut off by a rising tide of water, even as hordes of spectral figures begin to emerge out of the encroaching darkness. The theme park, it turns out, has been claimed by an expansive community of ghosts and spirits, and Chihiro can only rescue her parents by finding work in a bathhouse and servicing its supernatural clientele. *Spirited Away* is thus, literally, a story of enchantment, of shape-shifters, androgynous creatures, uncanny doubles, loquacious animals, and a gigantic baby the size of Colossus. But it is also a work that induces a sense of enchantment by exploiting the many-sided riches of anime as an imaginative and expressive medium.

In quintessential *Alice in Wonderland* fashion, the stout-hearted Chihiro stumbles across a variety of strange and surrealistic creatures during her quest, from the amiable to the curmudgeonly. Narrative suspense and surprise work their own particular magic, as the viewer's attention is held captive by the unexpected twists and turns of events: Chihiro's surprising encounters with the menacing matriarch Yubaba, the human-dragon hybrid Haku, the silent, shapeless spirit No Face. Yet the seductiveness of *Spirited Away* also pivots around its visual puns, glorious colors and exceptionally inventive and magical images. What remains in the mind is the comical grotesquerie of the portly, lumbering radish spirit; the Dante-esque inferno of the bathhouse boiler-room, its grizzly attendant frantically cranking wheels with his spider-like limbs; the vision of a magical train gliding silently below the water's surface with an assortment of shadows and specters on board. We are privy to strange associations and uncanny repetitions, a dream-like shifting and mutating of shapes as elements mysteriously decompose and recompose into new configurations. A trio of bouncing bodiless heads metamorphose into a giant baby, as the baby itself mutates into a perky mouse. What looks like a cloud of white birds turns out to be an assemblage of fluttering scraps of paper, which reassembles itself into an elderly woman, Yubaba's benign twin, decked out in the same vile turquoise eyeshadow. A massive, monstrous stink spirit, finally cleansed of oozing black slime and discarded junk, mutates into a diaphanous, benevolent, river god.

The visual radiance of such commercial art, even as it attracts both critical plaudits and appreciative audiences, is lost on critics adamant that authentic enchantment resides only in the pages of Shakespeare or Shelley. That a text is bankrolled by conglomerates or corporations tells us very little, in itself, about either its formal and artistic qualities or the aesthetic reactions it inspires. Economics can tell us a great deal about how cultures operate and reproduce themselves on a systemic level, yet it is a quite unreliable predictor of aesthetic response. A text's commodity status constitutes one facet of its existence, rather than being an all-determining essence that drains it, like an exceptionally diligent vampire, of all claims to beauty and aesthetic value.

Why, for example, do we so readily assume that a picture displayed on a museum wall will call forth a rich range of aesthetic responses and that the same image encountered in the pages of a magazine will only trigger a desire to buy more shoes? Such distinctions clearly have little to do with formal properties, with the visual qualities of the "text itself." Aesthetic theories – invocations of rapture, beauty, enchantment – turn out to rely on covert social theories – the conviction that the lives of those outside the charmed circle of Proust-lovers and art-show attendees are entirely bereft of such qualities. The phenomenological turns out, yet again, to be intertwined with the political. The conviction that popular art is nothing but a screen for ideological coercion stems in large part from a division of the disciplines that has stringently separated "art" from "culture." Selected works of art are shunted into the museum, where they are subjected to searching, many-sided interpretations and feted as the quintessential emblems of the aesthetic. What remains is held to embody purely instrumental use: the sating of crude psychic needs, the ideological manipulation of audiences, the utilitarian calculus of profit.[19] A continuum between high and popular art is twisted into a stark antithesis between beauty and ideology, between aesthetics and function, even as "literariness" is designated the one remaining source of salvation in a disenchanted world.

If enchantment is to be rendered a plausible concept for literary and cultural theory, it needs to be pried away from such a romantic-messianic vision and acknowledged as part of modernity rather than antithetical to modernity. It is difficult to discern any real difference between Greenblatt's description of being transfixed by the masterpieces on display at the Musée d'Orsay and Frankfurt School lamentations about shopgirls being mesmerized by Hollywood movies – apart, that is to say, from the pejorative adjectives with which the latter descriptions are decked out. What characterizes the phenomenology of enchantment simply is an intensely charged experience of absorption and self-loss. Given the sheer impossibility of getting inside someone's head to judge the quality of their aesthetic pleasure, any attempt to create a moral taxonomy of types of reader or viewer absorption – to make sweeping distinctions between authentic enchantment and baleful bewitchment – would appear to be based on little more than the reflexes of class prejudice.[20]

Manuel Puig's *Kiss of the Spider Woman* weaves an extended dialogue out of the words of two men incarcerated in an Argentine jail cell, the political revolutionary Valentin and the female-identified homosexual Molina. Molina entertains himself and his cell-mate by recounting the details of his favorite movies, spinning out painstaking renditions of assorted melodramas, romantic love stories, and horror films. While more than willing to go along with this exercise in mutual distraction, Valentin makes a point of keeping his distance, of underscoring that such films are far from his usual fare. As Molina dreamily spins out his stories, his cell-mate inserts an occasional ironic jibe or a nugget of Marxist or Freudian analysis. Valentin is the quintessential exponent of ideology critique, eager to demonstrate his fluency with theoretical codes, to translate aesthetic surfaces into hermeneutical depths, to diagnose the pathologies on display in the dream worlds of the culture industry.

The less educated Molina does not have the same ease with analytical terms; unable to come up with ready rejoinders to Valentin's debunking strategies, he can only lapse into sulking or silence. But Molina possesses a much greater eloquence when it comes to the act of retelling films, sliding easily from plot summary to the recounting of dialogue to elaborate visual descriptions. His relation to cinema is quintessentially aesthetic, attending to its formal and expressive qualities and the often indefinable emotions triggered by such qualities. Molina's renditions of movies pay attention to the textures of skin and the drape of fabrics, to chiaroscuro falls of light and shadow, to the extravagance and opulence of background sets and what they convey about character. Rather than reducing the films he describes to kernels of content, he dwells on the richness and resonance of visual details, striving to convey the quality of those moments when film freezes momentarily into the stillness and splendor of a tableau. "And now there's nothing but the moonlight coming in, and shining upon her, and she too looks like a statue so tall, with that white gown of hers that fits so tightly, looks like an ancient Greek amphora, with obviously the hips not too heavy, and a white scarf almost reaching the floor draped around her head, but without crushing her hairdo in the slightest, just framing it perfectly."[21]

Puig's novel is an exercise in aesthetic reeducation, as the Marxist militant who scorns commercial cinema is slowly seduced by the magic of Molina's storytelling. Even as Valentin surrenders some of his machismo and eventually becomes Molina's lover, so he opens himself up to the enchantment of movies that he once dismissed as sentimental kitsch. The realms of politics and popular art turn out to be not so far apart: Valentin's revolutionary beliefs are also re-demptive fictions, visions of hope and dreams of transcendence, no less mythical in their form than the dream worlds of mass culture. Engaging the art of film in a spirit of generosity and love, Puig's novel pays tribute to its affective intensities and magical powers. Drawing on B-movie prototypes to fashion its own love story between two doomed protagonists, *Kiss of the Spider Woman* fleshes out the many continuities across high and popular art.

The recently translated writings of Edgar Morin couple the allure of film to a series of broader meditations on magic and modernity. Like his fellow sociologist Michel Maffesoli, Morin is intrigued by manifestations of collective ecstasy, experiences of possession and rapture, explosions of intensity and affect. Permeating the culture of modernity, experiences of enchantment demand to be engaged in their own terms, as ritualized trance states tied to specific purposes and singular pleasures. The usual intellectual response of ideology critique can only result in a failed demystification: failed insofar as it is unable either to come to grips with the mysterious attraction of cinema or to dispel its powers.

In reflecting on this power, Morin writes: "what comes back once again . . . is the word *magic*, surrounded by a cortege of bubble words – marvelous, unreal, and so on – that burst and evaporate as soon as we try to handle them . . . They are passwords for what cannot be articulated."[22] As an analogy for the seductive power of film, magic allows us to recognize affinities between sacred and occult traditions and contemporary forms of commercial entertainment. In the movie theater the everyday world is represented yet also profoundly altered, haloed with an intensity of import and affective richness, in a modern reprise of the meaning-imbued world of animistic religions. Film also resuscitates the ancient fascination with doubles, the uncanny attraction of figures who are yet who are not us: ghostly alter egos and immortal images who flicker miraculously into life at the push of a button.

Yet the analogy is also imperfect, insofar as the context is entirely altered; magic is now removed from its practical, problem-solving functions in tribal or traditional life, reserved for the segregated and darkened space of the movie theater, transmuted into personalized, dream-like experiences of intense involvement. What cinema gives us, Morin points out, is a distinctive mélange of the magical, the affective, and the aesthetic. In its power to coat everyday things with luminosity and meaning, it ignites an intense connection between human beings and their world, reenchanting the realm of the seemingly disenchanted. The radiance of the screen image allows for an almost visceral experience of identification and absorption, a quasi-religious sense of being caught up in something greater than the self, of being bathed in the emotional intensity and vividness of dreams

Many of these same arguments also resonate with the experience of reading. The novel, for example, also haloes the things it describes with a plenitude of meaning, endowing them with an often exorbitant salience as harbingers of events or totemic objects. Hence its attempts to disenchant, to become a resolutely secular form, are only partially successful. Realism, too, is imbued with magic, in spite of its scientific and historical pretensions; it makes us see things, creates spellbinding fictions and special effects, specializes in hocus-pocus, pulls us into an imagined world as inexorably and absolutely as any work of fantasy. Moreover, while authors may strive to record the details of a social milieu with hard-headed precision, the objects that they invoke often assume an enigmatic, symbolic, even sacramental quality.[23] Novels give us the magic, as well as the mundanity, of the everyday; they infuse things with wonder, enliven the inanimate world, invite ordinary and often overlooked phenomena to shimmer forth as bearers of aesthetic, affective, even metaphysical meanings. It is not just that objects are haloed with the phantasmagorical allure of the commodity form, as the standard Marxist reading would have it. Capitalism may inflect or even intensify our sense of the magical, but in doing so, it latches onto affective predispositions and human yearnings that long predate modern economic systems.

Much of the critical animus against enchantment is fueled by a history of iconophobia, a longstanding fear and distrust of the image. For Marxist thinkers from Lukács to Debord, the truth-telling of narrative is diametrically opposed to the mystification of spectacle, as a form of idolatry or icon-worship stripped of all critical or historical awareness. Visual analogies dominate the commentary on literary enchantment, underscoring the uncanny power of words to conjure made-up worlds, to make us see what isn't there. Recent reclamations of the aesthetic often echo this view of the supreme irrationality of visual pleasure. Stephen Greenblatt contrasts art's ability to engender wonder – to transfix us and stop us in our tracks – with its power to create resonance – to generate a sense of the thickness of historical and cultural context. Resonance, he suggests, is tied to the transmission of voices and sound; wonder, by contrast, is linked to visual power and the mystique of the displayed object. Aesthetic rapture is made possible by a special kind of looking.[24]

And yet, to reflect on the etymology of enchantment is to be reminded of another kind of seduction: our propensity to be stirred by song, to be melted by music, to yield to the grain of the voice rather than the words that are spoken. It is the ear, rather than the eye, that epitomizes receptivity and vulnerability, as an orifice that can be penetrated from all directions, that cannot be closed at will, that can be invaded by the sweetest or the most unspeakable of sounds. Listening to music is often associated with a decentering or displacement of the self, a loss or blurring of ego boundaries, a sense of oceanic merging or pre-oedipal bliss. It is not especially surprising that some of the most eloquent descriptions of enchantment have come from critics writing on opera.[25]

The legend of the sirens famously symbolizes the seductiveness of sound. The sirens sing as reason sleeps, calling upon us to yield against our better judgment, to be moved beyond the boundaries of our rational awareness. In *The Dialectic of Enlightenment*, their song is read as catering to a pervasive desire for a "euphoric suspension of the self," embodying the narcotic intoxication and Dionysian bliss that lie at the origins of art.[26] The sirens epitomize the joys and the perils of self-loss, though in their later reflections on the sirenic lure of the culture industry, Adorno and Horkheimer will insist with uncompromising single-mindedess on the latter. To yield to the sirens is not simply to abandon one's will, but to hand it over to the control of outside forces. That music and the musicality of sound are so deeply entangled with notions of possession, of being occupied by an alien or supernatural power, underscores their pertinence to any genealogy and phenomenology of enchantment. This felt possession overcomes the poet, who gives voice to words she did not consciously intend, but also the reader or listener, moved by the sounds of these words in ways that he cannot consciously explain.[27]

Barthes, for example, speaks of a sensuous and embodied relation to words, invoking "language lined with flesh, a text where we can hear the grain of the throat, the patina of consonants, the voluptuousness of vowels, a whole carnal stereophony."[28] Such affinities with the sensual and quasi-tactile qualities of sounds also surface in my earlier reflections on falling in love with a style. These aural qualities are not only registered, but also recreated, in the minds of readers, who translate visual prompts into imagined aural patterns of intensity and stress, assonance and dissonance, timbre and tone. Sound effects can orchestrate associative states that float free of our usual cognitive and interpretive maneuvers, that respond subliminally to non-linguistic or para-linguistic stimuli.

Seamus Heaney speaks of the creation of soundscapes rather than landscapes, describing a form of affinity with poetry steered as much by musicality as by meaning, or rather, where meaning adheres to a poem's sonic effects as much as the things or themes to which it points. The notion of the soundscape underscores that attending to the materiality of language is far from synonymous with a soulless formalism; a soundscape is an auditory environment, a lived world composed of interwoven sound patterns that resonate inside and outside the self. Heaney refers to his own disinclination to follow a poem's conceptual progress, preferring, he writes, to "make myself an echo chamber for the poem's sounds."[29] In such cases, enchantment is triggered not by signifieds but by signifiers, not by mimetic identifications, but by phonic forms of expressiveness and their subliminal effects.

In his long poem/essay "Artifice of Absorption," language poet Charles Bernstein delves into the phenomenology of enchantment as well as the technical devices that enthrall, mesmerize, and engross readers. While unable to resist an occasional sideswipe at the mass media, Bernstein manages to sidestep the high-mindedness that is an occupational hazard of the avant-garde poetic statement. Instead, he adroitly interfolds ideas that all too often harden into sterile dichotomies: meaning versus its disruption or deferral, absorption versus impermeability, defamiliarization versus convention, enchantment versus knowingness. Bernstein intends to take absorption seriously, to ponder its role in realist works that call up imagined worlds as well in alternate forms – Romantic poetry, Poe's stories – that simulate the poignancy of memory or the intensity of dream. The seductive promise of causality or coherence serves as a lure for readers, Bernstein hypothesizes, as does the use of regular meter and repetition, with their lulling, hypnotic effects. Certain sub-genres – rhapsodic odes, poems of religious or romantic experience – pull out all the stops in welding absorptive lyric form with representations of rapturous states.

Such efforts can easily backfire, of course, resulting in unintended alienation effects that inspire only yawns or yelps of laughter. Conversely, realism and romantic poetry have no monopoly on reader involvement; enchantment is far from synonymous with transparency of form. Against much current critical dogma, Bernstein allows us to see that anti-absorptive devices are widely used for absorptive ends; artifice does not exclude immersion. He references Surrealism's use of strange juxtapositions and syntax to access a "deeper" reality, the Zaum poets' invention of incomprehensible words to create a quasi-magical state of aural trance; his own compositions. "In my poems, I / frequently use opaque & nonabsorbable / elements, digressions & / interruptions, as part of a technological / arsenal to create a more powerful / ("souped up") / absorption than possible with traditional, / & blander, absorptive techniques."[30] Literary theorists err when they equate innovative form with mental states of knowingness, irony, and distance. Linguistic experiments can accentuate rather than block involvement, using the musicality and expressiveness of sound to trigger inchoate yet intense associations or a sharpened auditory and sensory awareness. Bernstein allows us to see that absorption and artifice are often coterminous rather than mutually exclusive. The history of modern art is poorly explained as a story of intellectualization, a developmental arc away from affect and immersion toward ever greater levels of analytical self-consciousness. Rather, "the dynamic / of absorption is / central to all reading & writing."[31]

The case against enchantment has been fueled by two main charges: that it deludes and that it disables. What we might call the Madame Bovary problem is the fear that credulous persons, their reason befuddled and their senses bewitched, lose all ability to distinguish between real and imagined worlds. Much of the animus against enchantment stems from the belief that readers or viewers lack all discernment and critical judgment, mistaking beguiling fictions for historical truths. This animus, of course, is far from evenly distributed; while the critic routinely exempts himself from such confusion, he laments its effects on those groups deemed to have weaker powers of rational reflection, such as women and the lower classes.

Yet the experience of being immersed in a work of art involves a mental balancing act that is all too easily overlooked by critics quick to impute a dogged literalism onto imagined audiences. Even as we are bewitched, possessed, emotionally overwhelmed, we know ourselves to be immersed in an imaginary spectacle: we experience art in a state of double consciousness.[32] This is not to deny that imaginative fictions infiltrate and influence our lives, but to note that such a confluence rarely takes the form of a literal confusion of real and imagined worlds. A distinctive bifurcation of perception underlies modern aesthetic experience, whether "high" or "low"; even as we are enchanted, we remain aware of our condition of enchantment, without such knowledge diminishing or diluting the intensity of our involvement.

Michael Saler echoes this idea in invoking what he calls the ironic imagination: a pleasure in enchanted worlds that simultaneously acknowledges the imaginary nature of such worlds. In this sense, both high and popular art cater to a widespread yearning for wonder and mystery without denying modernity. Modern enchantments are those in which we are immersed but not submerged, bewitched but not beguiled, suspensions of disbelief that do not lose sight of the fictiveness of those fictions that enthrall us.[33] Such enchantments are magical without requiring the intervention of the supernatural, reminders of the persistence of the mysterious, wondrous, and perplexing in a rationalized and at least partly secularized world.

What, finally, should we make of enchantment's association with passivity, submission, and surrender? The condition of being totally absorbed by a book or a film is often expressed through images of being captured, caught up, held hostage. To speak of being overwhelmed by a text is to admit to a fervency and helplessness of response at odds with our usual sense of the knowing, self-possessed critic. Barry Fuller suggests that critics are drawn to the study of literature not only by the intellectual pleasures it offers, but also by "something swoonier, more embarrassing, some possible apprehension of sublimity or self-erasure in the presence of what is not ourselves."[34] This sense of something "swoonier, more embarrassing" is, as we have seen, often disavowed or directed onto the figure of the gullible or naïve reader. Yet it forms part of a long and diverse history of aesthetic, erotic, and religious practices that evidence a longing to loosen the fetters of consciousness, to experience the voluptuous and sometimes vertiginous pleasures of self-loss.

In one sense, to be sure, the appearance of passivity is misleading; any form of engagement with a work of art requires a modicum of interaction. Readers and viewers engage in covert yet complex acts of decoding, their brains silently buzzing away, carrying out complex forms of mental processing, drawing upon accumulated reservoirs of tacit knowledge. We are always involved in translating signs into imaginary scenarios, responding to subtle textual cues, filling in the blanks, elaborating and expanding on what a text gives us. There is a sense, moreover, in which we are also primed to experience enchantment by structures of pre-evaluation, including contextual clues, institutional norms, and ingrained expectations. The violin performance that inspires rows of rapt, dreamy faces in the concert hall encounters only stony or irritated expressions in the subway.[35]

And yet this crucial insistence on the social framing of aesthetic experience can obscure an equally salient truth: that we may feel taken hold of, possessed by a text in a way that we cannot entirely control or explain. If the reader has power, so too does a work of art, even as this power must remain latent until it is sparked into being by the dynamics of a particular encounter. Our education, our upbringing, our social position predispose us to certain cultural choices, yet there is often an unpredictability and surprise in the way that we feel ourselves claimed by some texts and left cold by others. That we can be pulled into the orbit of a work of art in a manner that feels momentous and mysterious is a phenomenological reality that should not be surrendered to conservative criticism.

Enchantment matters because one reason that people turn to works of art is to be taken out of themselves, to be pulled into an altered state of consciousness. While much modern thought relegates such hyper-saturations of mood and feeling to the realm of the child-like or the primitive, the accelerating interest in affective states promises a less prejudicial and predetermined perspective. The experience of enchantment is richer and more multi-faceted than literary theory has allowed; it does not have to be tied to a haze of romantic nostalgia or an incipient fascism. Indeed, enchantment may turn out to be an exceptionally fruitful idiom for rethinking the tenets of literary theory. Once we face up to the limits of demystification as a critical method and a theoretical ideal, once we relinquish the modern dogma that our lives should become thoroughly disenchanted, we can truly begin to engage the affective and absorptive, the sensuous and somatic qualities of aesthetic experience.

# 3

# *Knowledge*

What does literature know? The question of what literary texts reveal or conceal has been so emphatically hashed out that any further commentary seems hard-pressed to get beyond the desultory after-thoughts and caveats of epigones. Yet current conversations about mimesis and its correlates peter out, more often than not, in a dispir-iting sense of stalemate. Literary theorists feel obliged to pour cold water on commonsense beliefs about what texts represent, yet such purifying rituals are unable to dislodge a widespread intuition that works of art reveal something about the way things are. We can do justice to this intuition, and kick-start some stalled debates, by dis-puting the equation of reference with reflection and mimesis with mirroring. There are other ways of thinking about representation, models of mimesis that are attuned to the necessity of literary form rather than treating it as an irksome or intrusive impediment.

Canvassing the prevailing metaphors for capturing literature's claims to truth will give us a preliminary purchase on a vast archive. Perhaps the most persistent rendering of literature's relationship to the world is the figure of the semblance, shadow, or illusion, or analogously the counterfeit or imitation. Stretching back to Plato, complaints against the secondariness of art resound throughout the history of modernity, their most frequent target the scurrilous, duplicitous genre of the novel. Gaining a new lease of life in the twentieth-century practice of ideology critique, this same charge of mendacity drives the machinery of countless publications that inveigh against literary texts for dissembling the truth of social conditions.

The work of art, in this line of thought, is essentially a sham, a shameless un-truth, this failure of knowledge drawing all kinds of calamitous consequences in its wake, from the pollution of the polis to the creation of countless apologias for the inequities of capitalism.

Those anxious to force an admission of literature's revelatory powers, on the other hand, have often reached for the language of reflection, as in Stendhal's well-known rendering of the novel as a mirror promenading down the roadway capturing the insalubrious dirt and mud of the gutter as well as the light of the sky. Yet it did not take the Realists long to concede, in George Eliot's words, that the mirror of literature is defective, the reflection often faint or confused, and the goal of verisimilitude a daunting task. Another glassy image, the text as a window looking out on the world, was pressed into service by Ortega y Gasset, Henry James, Sartre, and others, while also doing duty within realist film theory, where it gestures toward an idea of perceptual objectivity freed of human prejudice. Both mirror and window metaphors have been roundly criticized for their presumption of transparency and for enshrining the supremacy of an eye-centered epistemology; the linguistic mediation of experience, it is argued, cannot help but place a massive dent in the credibility of all such visual analogies.

Marxist critic Georg Lukács is often hauled in as a whipping boy by critics railing against the naïveté of reflection theory. In reality, Lukács was fervently opposed to any aesthetic driven by ambitions of impartial copying or literal replication, insisting that any truly realistic art must be multi-layered, selective, and infused with the passions of the creator. The figure of the x-ray suggests itself as an analogy more suited to his conviction that the works of Balzac or Tolstoy penetrate below misleading surfaces and distracting details to disclose the dynamism of social processes. Even Stendhal's mirror offers a more complex analogy than is evident at first glance, as a dynamic and unstable reflector that offers a series of changing and inevitably partial views.[1] The stubborn persistence of referential commitments as well as the continuing pull of visual analogies resurface in the present-day vogue for cartographic metaphors, with Fredric Jameson's idea of cognitive mapping serving as the best-known example. The appeal to the map as a template for understanding alludes to the paradoxes of representation; that any attempt to capture social reality must be selective, that the writer who strives to capture everything will end up conveying nothing.

A second genealogy of images clusters around an expressive view of the artwork as an irradiating force whose luminous energies pulse out into the surrounding shadows. Shunning any notion of the literary work as a document of everyday contingencies, the figure of the lamp bears tribute to the power of poetic creativity in allowing us to apprehend truths previously unseen. This orchestrating motif of Romanticism is recharged and reinvigorated, yet rendered more somber, by the modern encounter with Freud and the vitalism of Nietzsche and Bergson. The truth afforded by art is now hailed as destabilizing and self-shattering, caught up in the demonic flux of unconscious desires, of an entirely different order to the data vouchsafed by science or the dulled and distracted perceptions of everyday life. Epiphany emerges as a signature mode of modernist aesthetics; the work of art discloses, makes manifest, forces into consciousness, what is otherwise inaccessible to thought. The exaltation of the artwork as a source of semi-sacred truth pivots on this claim that it transfigures and transforms, breaking through the crust of conventional schemata to call up new forms of consciousness, other ways of seeing.[2]

The question of art's epistemological status receded into the background during the heyday of New Criticism, when the literary text acquired the imperturbable aura of a verbal icon, charged with the task of being rather than meaning, described as "equal to, not true." Intent on elucidating the perplexities of poetic form, critics bracketed the question of what literature allows us to know or rebuffed such a question as encroaching on its immaculate self-sufficiency. While New Critics occasionally hazarded the view that poetic language most fully matched the many-shadedness of experience, such remarks were dropped in passing rather than woven into a substantial argument about literature and truth. By the time I entered graduate school in the early 1980s, however, literary studies had been freshly politicized and was firmly under the sway of Althusserian Marxism (whose impact, it must be said, was far greater in Europe and Australia than in the US). Althusserian critics scorned the sentimental attachment to bourgeois notions of truth that they discerned in the legacies of both realist and Romantic aesthetics. And yet, they were willing to toe the line of traditional aesthetic theory in one respect, conceding that the work of art is of a different order to run-of-the-mill ideology.

How, then, to explain this difference and justify this distinction? The metaphor of the symptom, with its medical and therapeutic associations, offered a way of capturing the status of the art object. Althusserian critics were adamant that literature cannot provide genuine knowledge, a possibility that they reserved for such explanatory sciences as Marxism or psychoanalysis. And yet, the argument went, it can attain a critical distance from the everyday work of ideology by rendering it in aesthetic form, thereby exposing its repressed or excluded meanings. "Literature challenges ideology" remarks Pierre Macherey, "by using it."[3] Just as the hysterical patient is racked by symptoms whose meanings and causes she cannot comprehend, so the literary text is riven by absences and fissures that call up social contradictions it cannot consciously address. The relationship between literature and the world is thus definitively recast; no longer iconic (based on putative likeness), it is now indexical (driven by a suppressed causality). Literary texts are unable to know themselves adequately, to grasp the social conditions that govern their existence, yet their symptomatic evasions and displacements, once diagnosed and traced back to their origins, afford insight into the forces that spawned them.

Althusserian theory was to ultimately fall victim to its own dwindling credibility, as Marxist pretensions toward objective knowledge were frayed by the collapse of really-existing socialism as well as multiplying criticisms of its political and methodological tenets. As wave after wave of intellectual skepticism washed over literary studies, as innumerable claims to truth were shipwrecked on the rock of deconstruction, critics struggled to find a foothold for making epistemological claims. If our perceptions of reality are always already steered by cultural contingencies and ideological prejudices, if our very grammar is imbued with arbitrary distinctions and self-referential figures, then the game of talking about truth has, it seems, conclusively played itself out. An entire cluster of terms – knowledge, reference, truth, mimesis – vanished from the higher altitudes of literary theory, if not from the workaday practice of teaching and criticism, admitted into *diacritics* or *Critical Inquiry* only when hedged around with an amplitude of scare quotes.

Yet the repressed was to reappear all too rapidly in the idea of literature as negative knowledge, as the opposite or antithesis of mimesis. We have returned in a sense to our starting point – the figuring of art as untruth – except that this negative appellation is now wrenched around to serve as a confirmation of literature's exemplary status. If all writing is beholden to the play of textuality rather than to criteria of fidelity or truthfulness, then literature is to be applauded for facing squarely up to its own fictional status, for refusing to pander to bogus criteria of objectivity and accuracy, and, in the case of modernist writing, for spurning commonsense criteria of legibility and narrative coherence. Rather than standing for idiosyncratic, atypical forms of language use, the literary work is catapulted to a position of symbolic centrality, as the ideal prism through which to apprehend the aesthetic and rhetorical features that subtend all acts of communication. In Paul de Man's often quoted words, "Literature is the only form of language free from the fallacy of unmediated expression."[4]

This viewpoint assumes a somber and even melancholic cast in the work of Adorno, where the negative knowledge afforded by the work of Kafka and Beckett is hailed as the only authentic, albeit bruised and impotent, option in a capitalist system that eviscerates language of all substantive content by commodifying and reifying every last word. It acquires a more blithe and untroubled expression in contemporary versions of Nietzscheanism, where critics delight in showing how literature chases its own tail in a never-ending *mise-en-abîme* or conjure subversion out of the ubiquitous idioms of theatricality and performance. Taking their cue from Roland Barthes, critics declared that realism in literature is nothing but a reality effect orchestrated by the play of language, and that writing is an intransitive verb that connotes but does not denote. The poetic function of language was promoted to its only function, as the "aboutness" of literature was deemed to center on literature itself. Conditions were now in place for a stream of critical readings proving that every conceivable text, from *The Wife of Bath* to *The Wizard of Oz*, was an auto-referential commentary on its own fictional status.[5]

This sequence of changing metaphors is often pitched as a chronicle of outgrown errors, as literary critics disembarrass themselves of the pesky metaphysical attachments that plagued their predecessors. Yet such attachments have turned out to be exceptionally resilient, clinging like limpets to the phrasing of those most anxious to shake them off. The assault on mimesis turns out to pivot on a series of knowledge claims, the denial of truth cannot help but hazard endless observations about how things really are. Philip Weinstein's recent advocacy for the state of "unknowing" espoused by modernist fiction, for example, consists of multiple speech acts of describing, analyzing, arguing, explaining, and judging. His account of how literature comes to wean itself from retrograde notions of truth and knowledge unfolds a negative teleology, engages in copious acts of historical generalization, and relies on numerous hypotheses about causality and influence. While Weinstein's readings are often illuminating, his larger argument is firmly anchored in those propositional and referential claims he seems most anxious to toss aside.[6] Indeed, in more than a few cases – most notably the chain of equivalence characteristic of much 1980s high theory, when realism, individualism, bourgeois culture, and capitalism were blithely conflated and condemned, such that any critique of Dickens or Dreiser did double duty as a heroic assault on the capitalist system – the truth claims of literary theorists turned out to be more totalizing than anything that nineteenth-century novelists could have dreamed of.

Looking back on this inglorious, if far from mute, moment in intellectual history, Christopher Prendergast and Antoine Compagnon observe that such flamboyant objections to literary mimesis have caricatured and misrepresented what mimesis entails.[7] Labeling the language of realism "transparent," for example, does a marked injustice to the metaphorical richness, semantic thickness, and polysemic density of many nineenth-century and twentieth-century novels. The claim that realism underwrites the dominant ideology by presenting culture under the sign of nature neglects its patently fictional, artful, and "make believe" aspects as registered by readers as well as authors. It also involves a not insignificant dollop of bad faith, given that such accusations are anchored in referential assertions, causal hypotheses, and social diagnoses that replicate the very structures of thought that are being disavowed.

The question of literature's relationship to knowledge remains open; much will depend, of course, on how we define the act of knowing. In my first chapter, I focused on literature's potential merits as a guide to self-interpretation and self-understanding. I now turn to what literature discloses about the world beyond the self, to what it reveals about people and things, mores and manners, symbolic meanings and social stratification. Not all texts, of course, lend themselves equally well to such an analytical rubric; my concluding chapter centers on works that actively defy or disrupt our frameworks of social reference. But one motive for reading is the hope of gaining a deeper sense of everyday experiences and the shape of social life. Literature's relationship to worldly knowledge is not only negative or adversarial; it can also expand, enlarge, or reorder our sense of how things are.

This repertoire of sense-making devices is firmly anchored in the formal and generic properties of literary texts. Marjorie Perloff draws a mistaken, if not uncommon, conclusion when she asserts that "if the main purpose of a literary text is to convey knowledge or formulate truth, questions of form and genre take a back seat."[8] In reality, knowledge and genre are inescapably intertwined, if only because all forms of knowing – whether poetic or political, exquisitely lyrical or numbingly matter-of-fact – rely on an array of formal resources, stylistic conventions, and conceptual schemata. The category of genre pertains not just to literature or art but to all communication, given that meaning is indelibly shaped by the structure and the situation of utterances. The lab report, the political speech, the deconstructive essay, the folk tale, are all generic forms that fashion specific effects of truth and plausibility, authority and persuasiveness.[9] As sociologists of knowledge and philosophers of language have long attested, cognition is not a passive recording or imprinting on the psyche but an active selecting, ordering, and shaping of material, a means of making intelligible. In this sense, form and genre are not an impediment to knowledge, but the only conceivable means of attaining it.

Recent critiques of literature's referential ambitions, it is sometimes noted, betray the signs of a frustrated idealism in their lingering attachment to an ideal of absolute comprehensiveness. Works of literature are taken to task for displaying signs of partiality and limitedness, chastised for their acts of exclusion. If we take on board the idea that all forms of knowing are shaped by the constraining and enabling conventions of genre, including the critic's own, such complaints risk sliding into the realm of tautology. That literary works yield limited perspectives does not prevent them from also serving as sources of epistemic insight. In this regard, we should be wary of yoking genres too tightly to a particular epistemology by presuming, for instance, that realism strives to master and map the world, whereas modernism testifies to an unalloyed crisis of knowledge and representation. Mimesis, in the manner I define it here, is by no means limited to realism but extends to instances of modernism, poetry, and postmodern prose. Once we relinquish the false picture of a reality "out there" waiting to be found, we can think of literary conventions as devices for articulating truth rather than as obstacles to its discovery.

Here I am indebted to the work of Paul Ricoeur, especially his invitation to think of mimesis as a redescription rather than a reflection, a chain of interpretive processes rather than an echo or an imitation. This bid for redefinition is grounded in a return to Aristotle's conception of mimesis as an act of making rather than copying.[10] Our experience of the world is always, in Ricoeur's terms, *pre-figured*; embedded in a plenitude of symbolic practices, social competences, and discursive repertoires. The world against which we measure the truth claims of the literary text is a world that is already mediated via stories, images, myths, jokes, commonsense assumptions, scraps of scientific knowledge, religious beliefs, popular aphorisms, and the like. We are eternally enmeshed within semiotic and social networks of meaning that shape and sustain our being. Hence it makes no sense to conjure up some notion of things as they really are – some higher altitude stripped bare of all symbolization and sense-making – against which we could measure the truth claims of the literary work.

This semiotic material is in turn *configured* by the literary text, which refashions and restructures it, distancing it from its prior uses and remaking its meanings. Mimesis, then, is an act of creative imitation, not mindless copying, a strenuous shaping, distilling, and reorganizing of texts and experiences. Here Ricoeur allots a singular importance to narrative as a staple of our cultural grammar, an indispensable means of connecting persons, things, and coordinates of space and time. Rejecting a line of thought that decries plot as a deceptive device masking an unformed temporality, he points out that we have no possible access to time "in itself" and that any conception of time as a chaotic and meaningless flux is itself a fiction spun out of quintessentially modernist preoccupations. Conversely, plotting does not signal the sovereignty of a singular order of truth, but embraces contingencies, reversals, and variations of complex and often unexpected kinds. To be sure, we can question the politics built into certain storylines, as feminist critics have done in relation to the Victorian novel, but our conceptions of politics, literature, human relations, the interaction between social structures and human agency, remain deeply beholden to the logic of narrative.[11]

Ricoeur's recasting of mimesis opens up an amplitude of ways of rethinking representation that extend far beyond his own focus on temporality and narrative. Literary works draw on a multiplicity of mimetic devices to achieve their effects, of which I highlight three; deep intersubjectivity, ventriloquism, and the linguistic still life. In each case, *vraisemblance* is created through patently artful means, by drawing on a repertoire of formal resources. The literary work reworks the work of culture, redescribes the already described; it involves, to borrow a happy phrase from ordinary language criticism, not the correspondence of words to things, but the illumination of words by words.[12]

Yet this network of linguistic cross-references is far from solipsistic or self-enclosed; language gestures incessantly beyond itself, hazarding claims about the way things are. Our uses of words are tangled up with our embeddedness in the world; our relations with people and things are intimately intertwined with practices of knowing. While material realities cannot ground patterns of sense-making that fluctuate dramatically within and across cultures, such realities nevertheless impinge on what and how we know, set up resistances to our conceptual schemes or prompt us to reassess our beliefs. In this sense, it is entirely possible to speak of the referential function of language without positing a correspondence theory of truth or an extra-linguistic reality directly accessible to human understanding. Ricoeur shares with Rorty a fondness for the idiom of redescription, yet without ruling out of court all talk of knowledge or reference. Literary redescriptions engage us not simply because they are surprising or seductive, but also because they can augment our understanding of how things are.

What exactly is Ricoeur's phrase "mimesis as metaphor" intended to convey? Mimesis performs an analogous cognitive function to metaphor, proposes Christopher Prendergast in a helpful gloss; they are modes of active disclosure, discovery procedures, dynamic redescriptions of the world.[13] Metaphor, like fiction, consists of statements that are counterfactual, that are not literally true. Yet that metaphors invoke non-existent state of affairs does not make them misguided or mistaken; they serve as a means of "seeing as," invite us to see things differently rather than reporting on what is empirically the case. What metaphor and mimesis share is the capacity to generate new perspectives, to make possible other ways of seeing, to intensify meaning by dynamically recreating a world already mediated by language. That something is a figure of speech does not disqualify it from also serving as a source of potential truth. Along with other theorists of metaphor, Ricoeur insists that cognition and metaphor are welded together, that we cannot help but make sense of the world through models and poetic analogies. Literary mimesis is an intensifying of modes of creativity already alive in language, rather than an attachment to wrong-headed notions of impartial copying.

The third element of mimesis in Ricoeur's schema is *transfigura-tion*, the work's impact upon the reader. The work only comes to life in being read, and what it signifies cannot be separated from what readers make of it. Mimesis is thus recast as a tri-partite rather than a dualistic structure, with reception as vital as production. Yet the idea of transfiguration suggests that readers are not fully knowable and foreseeable, that they cannot be boxed into the sum of their demo-graphic data, that they exist in a state of becoming rather than being. Over time, readers are shaped by what they read, even as they can-not help but impose on texts what they already know. Here again we can apprise the relevance of genre, not as a rigid set of formal rules, but as flexible criteria that we impute or ascribe to texts. Whether the works of Edith Wharton are approached as novels of manners, works of naturalist fiction, or contributions to a tradition of women's writing, for example, will surely affect what readers are likely to glean from them.

Wharton, in fact, offers a good test case for working through some relations between literary and other forms of knowledge. *The House of Mirth* details the lifestyles of fashionable and wealthy New Yorkers at the turn of the century, as it narrates the inexorable decline of the elegant and well-bred Lily Bart. Equipped with a love of luxury yet financially straitened, Lily stumbles repeatedly in her efforts to find a wealthy husband, sinking through the strata of New York life to an ignominious and lonely death in a dingy boarding house. Wharton is often hailed as a literary ethnographer intent on rendering the minute details of milieu and moment, bringing to vivid life the Byzantine rituals, unspoken protocols, and covert snobberies and cruelties of New York high society. Her work is infused with ideas drawn from the nascent field of anthropology and its conception of culture, drawing on ethnographic assumptions to contextualize the lives of ordinary people by placing them within "an elaborate stage-setting of manners, furniture, and costume," underscoring how the outer worlds of her characters impinge on and mold their inner lives.[14]

Those critics most anxious to defend the value of literature are inclined to brush off what they call the merely historical aspects of a text, where "merely historical" refers to the contingent and particular details of time and place. Even if works of literature can tell us something about past lives, the argument goes, this tells us nothing about their value as literature, given that such a task can just as easily be carried out by historians. Historical knowledge is, in other words, not what sets literature apart, not the source or measure of its distinctiveness, and cannot command the serious attention of the literary critic. Charles Altieri drives home the point when he writes: "literature seems too important to culture not to be seen as conveying some kind of knowledge, yet if we put too much analytic pressure on the forms of representation literature offers, we may well lose its special qualities and treat it only as inferior social science, psychology, or philosophy."[15]

In practice, however, such arguments often beg the question of what counts as historical knowledge and pay scant attention to the particularities of genre. Such knowledge may depend on, rather than diverge from, the distinctive qualities of literary form. Wharton, for example, gives us a microscopic rendering of what we might call, in Wittgensteinian terms, forms of life. *The House of Mirth* zeroes in on the tacit knowledge, commonplace gestures, modes of conduct, and totemic objects that make up a particular culture or subculture. Wharton shows how a tone of voice, a lifted eyebrow, a chance meeting, the appearance or absence of a party invitation, can spell out social success or a precipitous drop into the void. She investigates structures of feeling, probes the contours of unspoken assumptions, captures the figures of speech and filaments of thought through which a world is appraised and understood, draws out the innumerable principles of distinction around which a particular culture organizes itself. We come to recognize the object that we often, all too vaguely, call society, not as being opposed to the particular, but as reproducing itself through the accretion of endless particulars, through the steady accumulation of everyday events, fleeting observations, and microscopic judgments.

How, a skeptic might object, does any of this differ from what a historian might accomplish, especially now that history has shifted away from the study of diplomatic maneuvering and world historical battles toward cultural history and the study of *mentalités*? Or from an anthropologist's or sociologist's scrutiny of the norms, rituals, and practices through which a society reproduces itself? Indeed, to scan the criticism on *The House of Mirth* is to come across copious references to Veblen and Marx, to material culture and feminist theories of the gaze, as scholars draw out commonalities between Wharton's endeavor and various theses drawn from critical theory and the social sciences. What, then, does Wharton's novel tell us that a work of history or sociology cannot?

A novel such as *The House of Mirth* unfolds a social phenomenology, a rendering of the qualities of a life-world, that is formally distinct from either non-fiction or theoretical argument. These textual markers put paid to the assumption that there are no meaningful formal distinctions between literary and non-literary genres, refuting, for example, the observation that "viewed simply as verbal artifacts, history and novels are indistinguishable from each other."[16] Such claims draw their force from the analysis of narrative; in the wake of the linguistic turn it was widely acknowledged that historical writing, rather than delivering unvarnished accounts of things as they really were, drew heavily on archetypal plot structures and rhetorical figures. The term "fiction" subsequently acquired a new currency as a catch-all term used to describe both factual and imaginative writing, often with the express intent of effacing the differences between them.

While the plots of history and fiction share certain features, however, the novel is distinguished at the level of discourse in various ways, including, most notably, its ability to read minds. Third person fiction allows the narrator an epistemological privilege that accrues neither to real life nor to the writing of history: unrestricted access to the inner life of other persons. Referencing this experience of mind-reading – which surfaces across a swathe of realist and modernist texts – Dorrit Cohn draws attention both to its sheer strangeness and the lack of sustained theoretical analysis it has received. Fiction is the only medium in which the interiority of persons is promiscuously plumbed, where narrators routinely know more about the minds of characters than they know themselves. Bound by criteria of verifiable evidence, historians reference the inner lives of their subjects only when authorized to do so by letters, diaries, or memoirs; the protocols of historical research require that other forays into interiority be clearly marked as speculative. Even when history verges on biography, it draws on a language of conjecture and induction rooted in referential documentation that differs significantly from the discourse of novels.[17] Precisely because of the epistemological shakiness of fiction, its freedom to ignore empirical criteria and constraints of evidentiary argument, it offers an initiation into the historical aspects of intersubjectivity that is unattainable by other means.

In the opening chapter of *The House of Mirth*, for example, Wharton steers her protagonist, Lily Bart, through a chain of revelatory episodes, from a chance encounter at the train station with her friend, Lawrence Selden, to the drinking of afternoon tea at Selden's apartment, to an awkward conversation with another acquaintance, the banker Simon Rosedale, who catches sight of her as she is leaving Selden's building. The text's shuttling between inner and outer worlds, its blending of social documentation with small-scale dramas of perception and reaction, engenders a distinctive optic. Our first description of Lily is focalized by Selden, whose gaze drifts surreptitiously across her facial features as they walk together down the street: "the modelling of her little ear, the crisp upward wave of her hair – was it ever so slightly brightened by art? – and the thick planting of her straight black lashes." We are inculcated into a particular way of seeing, a blazon-like inventory and judicious assessment of female body parts. These flitting fragments of perception dissolve into a semi-conscious mélange of interpretations and judgments: "he had a confused sense that she must have cost a great deal to make, that a great many dull and ugly people must, in some mysterious way, have been sacrificed to produce her." Wharton's heroine is situated from the start in economies of exchange, in calculations of cost and value that are intertwined with, rather than distinct from, the aesthetic delight that she triggers in her admirers.[18]

Selden's musings tell us a great deal about Lily, but also about Selden himself: they gesture, from the start, toward a social system that allots unmarried women of a certain class a specific and tightly restricted field of movement, while filling out this broader scheme with the semi-conscious perceptions, fallible interpretations, and fleeting interactions of the individuals embedded within it. We become conscious of Lily's staging of her own presence as an exquisite *objet d'art*, but also of the ways in which Selden's own proclivities incline him toward a wry and detached assessment of her aesthetic qualities. In other words, we come to see Lily as she is seen by others, as she is knotted into a fabric made up not just of the discourses and social norms that tend to command the attention of historicist critics, but also of subtle affinities, gazes of complicity, blushes of shame or agitation, tactful evasions and pregnant silences, inchoate stirrings of desire or distaste, what we might call, in Nathalie Sarraute's term, "tropisms": an elaborate, if often subterranean choreography of perception and emotion, of reaction and involvement, that plays itself out in and across the social field.

What Wharton's novel gives us, then, is not just anthropology, but phenomenology: a literary rendering of how worlds create selves, but also of how selves perceive and react to worlds made up of other selves. Emancipated from criteria of verifiable accuracy, her writing is free to register fleeting expressions, penumbral perceptions, shifting foci of attention, subconscious motions of affinity and distancing: all the ephemeral and barely registered forms of consciousness and communication that help make up the stuff of social interaction. George Butte coins the phrase "deep intersubjectivity" to denote this capturing of the intricate maze of perceptions, the changing patterns of opacities and transparencies, through which persons perceive and are perceived by others. Deep intersubjectivity gives us representations of persons neither as solipsistic Enlightenment monads nor empty linguistic signifiers but as embedded and embodied agents, mediated yet particular, formed in the flux of semiotic interchange. We are drawn into a world in which gazes meet or avoid other gazes, verbal tones and inflections weave subterranean dialogues, and bodies encircle and encounter each other in space.[19]

Such a rendering of intersubjectivity has broader theoretical and philosophical resonances, revealing, for example, intriguing parallels to Wittgenstein's and Cavell's ruminations on the possibility of knowing other minds.[20] Yet it also enriches and deepens our sense of history and habitus, of *mentalité* and modes of sociability. The act of reading often calls for a cross-temporal leap, a destabilizing shift from one time frame and cultural sensibility to another. How do we negotiate the details of this transhistorical encounter, one as fraught, in its own way, as the meeting of ethnically and racially diverse cultures in the present?

The technique of deep intersubjectivity instantiates a view of particular societies "from the inside"; we come to know something of what it feels like to be inside a particular habitus, to experience a world as self-evident, to bathe in the waters of a way of life. By attending to the salience of what is said and what is left unsaid, by reading looks and gestures, attending to half-voiced thoughts and inchoate sensations, we become attuned to criteria of distinction that seem at first glance to be baffling or opaque, that may surprise us in their sheer arbitrariness. *The House of Mirth* does not just depict a network of social discriminations and judgments, it also enfolds readers, through its inculcation of countless examples, into an experiential familiarity with the logic of such judgments, with what we might call a feel for the game. Nothing in Wharton's work suggests that she is endorsing the mores of the society that she describes – her perspective on New York tribal cultures tends toward the severe, even sardonic. Yet the simulation of forms of life through techniques of deep intersubjectivity also works against readers' attempts to distance themselves from past cultures – to judge them peremptorily as backward or benighted – by bringing them unnervingly close.

In this sense, while Wharton's fiction cannot replace the diagnostic tools of Marx or Veblen, neither can it be replaced by them; it gives us a social world in a different key, it opens up what Alfred Schutz calls the meaning-contexts of a milieu, it unfolds the meaningfulness of a world as it is lived by its inhabitants.[21] As a means of knowing, it veers away from the classic idea of epistemology as the correct representation of an independently given reality. An attunement to the microscopic subtleties of social interaction has often been deemed the province of women and not infrequently dismissed as intuitive, impressionistic, or overly subjective. As a form of context-sensitive knowledge conveyed to readers, it is more akin to *connaître* than *savoir*, "seeing as" rather than "seeing that," learning by habituation and acquaintance rather than by instruction. And yet the paradox lies in this sense of realness being achieved through artful means, with literature's epistemological license allowing it to convey a uniquely multi-layered sense of how things are. In this sense, the reactions that readers sometimes have to imaginary characters – that we know them better than people in real life – is not a naïve misjudgment, but an entirely accurate perception, fostered by simulations of intersubjectivity that offer unparalleled access to the mental worlds of other persons and the subterranean complexities of their interactions.

Of course, such a speculative exercise in social phenomenology can fumble or fail, sometimes in spectacular fashion. It is not difficult to think of cases where authorial forays into mind-reading fail to ring true, or when an otherwise subtle rendering of motivations and manners halts, in sheer perplexity or casual indifference, at the threshold of certain interiorities. Rendered as social allegories or assumed unworthy of scrutiny, entire categories of persons – servants, those of non-Western origin, the working class – were long relegated to the status of minor characters in fiction, their social standing converted into a damning aesthetic judgment. That all fictional renderings of personhood are shaped by power-driven relations of blindness as well as insight seems incontrovertible. In an ingenious argument, however, Alex Woloch proposes that this patent unevenness of novelistic attention, the disproportionate space allotted to major and minor characters, does not blindly acquiesce to prevailing prejudice, but exposes and comments on it. The effacement or the asymmetrical treatment of persons in fiction, their routine rendering as flat or one-dimensional types, is a means by which the novel registers and reflects on the pervasiveness of social hierarchies.[22]

Tracing the psychodynamics of intersubjectivity is one means by which literature registers its worldly concerns. What of its talent for ventriloquism, for imitating idioms, delving into dialects, echoing the tics and mannerisms of styles of speech? Mimesis is closely related to mimicry; a concept that appears to hinge on visual analogy also incorporates verbal imitation, linguistic echoes, and a panoply of oral and auditory associations. Literary texts often contain renditions of multiple voices and heteroglot languages, stealing words from other sources in order to make them issue as if by magic, from their own mouths. Immersing themselves in a sea of linguistic styles and registers, they draw attention to idiosyncratic and idiomatic word choices, highlight the rhythms and cadences, stutters and stresses, the quasi-tactile and tangible qualities of particular types of speech. One way literature makes us think is through its exercise of verbal virtuosity, its demand that we adapt our minds to multiple lexicons and modes of expression that encompass alternative ways of making sense of experience.

Such observations bring to mind heavily canvassed Bahktinian themes of polyphony and heteroglossia, yet in the current critical scene such themes are often eviscerated of any determinate content and watered down into reassuring bromides about the dialogic or subversive qualities of novelistic form. Heteroglossia, however, describes the moment when linguistic distinctions match up with socio-ideological ones, when historical divisions are actualized and verbalized in unique configurations of lexis, grammar, and style.[23] Such utterances can highlight patterns of social stratifications, forcing us to see how linguistic distinctions match up with political ones, how words partake of asymmetrical and unequal worlds. Ventriloquism thus shifts into an emphatic, if indirect, means of social commentary.

While literary forays into non-standard English were once clearly marked as anomalous, with the home-spun homilies of coster-mongers or cab-drivers framed by a narrator's formal prose, writers are now whole-heartedly embracing a wide variety of linguistic idioms, immersing readers in multiple varieties of what Evelyn Chi'en calls "weird English."[24] We need only think of the flamboyant Anglo-Indianisms of Rushdie or the rebarbative, expletive-filled prose of Irvine Welsh or James Kelman. Rather than being safely confined within a fictional universe, such differences announce themselves forcefully, even intrusively, as readers strive to make sense of unfamiliar idiolects, grappling with modes of expression that seem eccentric or strange. This rhetoric of selective, socially differentiated understanding, as Doris Sommer calls it, conspires to rebuff complacent or impatient readers, underscoring how asymmetries of culture and politics can slow down or stall communication. The point is not to announce some general epistemological crisis but to make manifest how forms of knowing are tied up with distinctive ways of thinking and speaking that resist translation.[25]

Australian author Tim Winton has drawn attention to the obstacles of writing in a global marketplace, as British and American editors urge him to tone down his local idiom to increase his marketability. "I always wanted to use Australian vernacular; just paste it on until it ceased being commonplace and became poetic," Winton comments in an interview; "there has always been that stream in our literature but in the past 15 years we have been desperately trying to be international and desperately trying not to turn anyone off."[26] While such use of local vernacular may rebuff some readers, it has also helped to make Winton a prominent figure in the field of Australian literature, with its increasing appetite for literary explorations of national and regional identity. Even as his words blurt out their location, bear witness to their antipodean origins, they underscore the flimsiness of any dichotomy between poetic language and everyday speech. The minutiae of working-class lives are realized through an elaborate repertoire of verbal devices; what is portrayed becomes inseparable from the words used to portray it; immersion in the taste and texture of local idiom becomes a precondition of knowing and understanding a way of life. To open a book by Winton is to be forced into consciousness of the thickness and presence of language, as both a barrier and an opening to other worlds. We are faced with a social phenomenology cast in a purposefully linguistic key, where the apprehension of a life-world is inseparable from the words in which it is expressed.

At the center of Winton's *Cloudstreet*, for example, stands a house that is uncannily animate, that sighs and groans and shudders, that the characters try to leave but to which they inevitably return. Set in Perth from the 1940s to the 1960s, the novel centers on the lives of two families, the Pickles and the Lambs, who live in separate halves of a ramshackle old mansion that the Pickles have unexpectedly inherited. It is not far-fetched to think of language as another dwelling place in the novel, as a force that shelters and gathers together its inhabitants. Its bricks and mortar are colloquialisms, slang, vulgarities, Australianisms, passing observations and clichés, assembled into a shape of experience that is both familiar and strange. Winton ventriloquizes the local love of abbreviations (beaut, journo) and draws heavily on slang (dunny, chunder, grog, ratbag); regional references abound (the Anzac club, Freo, laughing like a flock of galahs). Spelling and punctuation are often modified to convey the quality of local accents and intonation: "Its orright, Fish. / Doan cry." Yet *Cloudstreet* is far from a literal-minded record of colloquialisms or an earnest ethnographic document. In Ricoeur's terms, Winton reconfigures the shape of everyday language, takes over and transforms the words he hears through techniques of selection, concentration, and stylization.[27]

Here syntax and structure are decisive; language erupts onto the page in sporadic fits and spurts, as a textual weave of staccato rhythms and disjointed patterns helps to fashion a sense of cut-to-the-chase brusqueness. The abruptness often associated with Australian working-class speech is intentionally heightened and transmuted into an overarching aesthetic device; dialogues composed of terse interchanges, each response a mere two or three words long, succeed each other the full length of a page, stranded in a sea of whiteness, like found poems crystallizing out of the detritus of everyday conversations. Much of Winton's text is spun out of juxtaposed snippets of conversations and reported speech; as this dialogue is frequently unattributed, it is difficult to discern exactly who is speaking, to distinguish one speaker from another in a colloquy of voices. The effect is akin to the anonymous collective wisdom of a Greek chorus rather than the clearly individuated figures of realist fiction. Since Winton steers clear of quotation marks, elements of dialogue, description, and narrative commentary fuse together, intermingling the narrator's words with the utterances of those whose stories he is telling. One scene dissolves rapidly into the next, characters are often laconically designated as "he" or "you," without further explanation: words appear mysteriously as if out of nowhere, rising to the surface without identity or attribution.

Winton's rendering of vernacular languages and ordinary experiences falls outside the usual protocols for portraying such lives, stripped of the ethnographic condescension that often frames descriptions of the poor, whose being is defined and peremptorily dispatched through a predictable calculus of social causality. Even as subtle shades of class and cultural difference unfold in how people speak or remain silent, the working-class lives portrayed in *Cloudstreet* fail to yield up their mysteries. Mrs. Lamb inexplicably flees her house and sets up a permanent home in a tent in the backyard; the family pig appears to be speaking in tongues; various rooms turn out to be peopled by phantoms and strange forces. The metaphysical folds into the physical, the numinous unveils itself in the everyday, even as vernacular idiom is exposed in all its comedy, beauty, and strangeness.

"Will you look at us by the river!" Winton begins. "The whole restless mob of us on spread blankets in the dreamy briny sunshine skylarking and chiacking about for one day, one clear, clean, sweet day in a good world in the midst of our living." We are plunged without ado into the midst of things, drawn into what sounds like a colloquial monologue or conversation. And yet the ordinariness of the opening phrase is belied by what follows: "mob" is a common enough style of self-designation in everyday Australian English, but "dreamy briny sunshine," in spite of its simplicity, shades into the poetic. And what on earth is chiacking? When the mysterious "staggerjuice" appears immediately afterward ("There's gingerbeer, staggerjuice, and hot flasks of tea"), one starts to feel that Winton is laying it on too thick, pasting on obscure or obsolete Australianisms to make a point. Yet the general drift is evident enough, even as such verbal concoctions underscore the very fine line that separates ordinary colloquialisms from Joycean wordplay. Like the odd nicknames acquired by the various protagonists, everyday language turns out to be imbued with unexpectedly strange and surreal elements.

Winton recreates a way of life less by probing how people feel than by immersing us in how they talk. His circumspection about interiority mimics that of his characters, whose language is laconic and unsentimental, joking or brusque, impatient with perceived pretension, spilling out in crescendos of insults or clipped rhythms of repartee. *Cloudstreet* orients its readers through acts of linguistic mimicry, immersing them in idioms that fall outside the repertoire of standard English and that convey something of the pervasive if largely unconscious patterns of experience – the cultural grammar – through which particular lives are lived. Language acquires an aesthetic thickness, an intonational concreteness, that speaks to its rootedness in a particular milieu and moment. This is social knowledge transmitted in a distinctively linguistic key; not through a slavish imitation of vernacular expression, but through stylized recreations of such expression that cause new meanings to unfold.

Phenomenology is often perceived as a philosophy of things, as a patient and purposeful turning toward the object. What might literary texts teach us about the social resonance of stuff? How do works of art reorient us toward the material world? In the not too distant past, objects held captive in poetry or prose were routinely vaporized and dematerialized by critics, stripped of their seeming solidity and put firmly in their proper place as signifiers referring to other signifiers. Literary theorists poured scorn on anyone rash enough to profess that words referred to material entities, a view of language widely felt to be backward and benighted. At present, however, objects are basking in the light of a newfound attention. Though words indisputably link up to other words, critics now concede, they may also speak of the secret lives of things, reveal something of the mute matter to which they gesture.

The nineteenth-century novel springs to mind as the quintessential archive of objects, a genre that obsessively lists, catalogues, itemizes, describes, and piles up stuff. In his recent reappraisal of the realist novel, Peter Brooks suggests that one of its main tasks is to fashion a phenomenological inventory of the world. What is irreducible in the realist project, he writes, is its ambition to register the importance of the things – objects, inhabitations, accessories – amid which people live.[28] To open a novel by Balzac, Dickens, or Zola is to encounter a cornucopia of objects, a plenipotentiary of wares, enumerated and elaborated in all their historical distinctiveness and material density. The bourgeoning interest in material culture and everyday life, ventures Brooks, makes us more sympathetic to the ambitions of nineteenth-century novelists, less willing to go along with high modernist condescension toward Victorian bric-à-brac and over-stuffed novels.

Elaine Freedgood offers a less sanguine view of such ordinary objects, arguing that the novel's relation to the history of things is deeply qualified and compromised. Because of its rush to subordinate objects to subjects, to exploit material things by pressing them into service as metaphorical extensions of character, the novel offers us only tantalizing glimpses and foreshortened histories of those same objects. Its optic is willfully shortsighted, obscuring the ugly episodes of conflict and conquest that underlie the presence of mahogany furniture in *Jane Eyre* or the appearance of tobacco in *Great Expectations*. Freedgood asks us to take objects literally, to read metonymically rather than metaphorically, following novelistic things beyond the covers of novels to capture something of their complex histories.[29]

How do we adjudicate between the spheres of consumption and production, or, more specifically, phenomenology and political economy? Is the import of an object bound up with the history of its making, or in the meanings that are subsequently bestowed upon it? To attend to a thing in its sensuous particularity, its sheer manifest presence, is to overlook the prior acts of production and exchange that have brought it to its current resting place. Description, as Lukács famously concluded, all too easily impedes or thwarts narration. Politically minded critics often treat the painterly or poetic still life with notable severity, accusing it of concealing history, denying contingency, and immobilizing time. And yet something may also be gained from a temporary staying of motion, from pausing to attend fully and whole-heartedly to a thing. Indeed, what draws together the diverse arguments in the field of "thing theory" is a sense that the most established critical language for talking about things – namely Marxism – suffers from an overly censorious relationship toward its object. Reification and fetishism have given things a bad name.

"I have a crazy / crazy love of things," writes Pablo Neruda in his exuberant "Ode to Things." He continues: "many things conspired / to tell me the whole story. / Not only did they touch me, / or my hand touched them: / they were / so close / that they were a part / of my being / they were so alive with me / that they lived half my life / and will die half my death."[30] Looking askance at the belief that only natural phenomena or animate beings merit our affections, he invokes an "irrevocable river of things," takes a close look at the everyday wares and mass-produced products that clutter up our lives, pauses in wonder before thimbles and brushes, vases and hats. While a lifelong communist, Neruda does not see such commercial stuff as a prototypical allegory of modern alienation but as matter alive with meaning, irreducibly other, yet woven deep into the very fabric of our being. He speaks of "objects / that I secretly covet," admits to being seduced, dazzled, and captivated by things, "that one there for its deep-sea color / and that one for its velvet feel." In several volumes of verse published during the 1950s, he pays homage to the most ordinary and overlooked items: scissors, a pair of socks, onions, chairs, tomatoes, spoons, a bar of soap, French fries.

Poems, of course, often strive to approximate objects, to mimic motionless matter, to simulate a state of solidity and self-containedness. When a thing makes manifest another thing, we would seem to have reification squared, a mode of aesthetic expression doubly stripped of social resonance and historical embedding. Studies of what Germans call the *Dinggedicht*, in its variants from Rainer Maria Rilke to William Carlos Williams, often stress its hermeticism, its adherence to a chiseled, water-tight structure that suspends motion and freezes the flux of historical time. And yet the poetics of still lives is not necessarily opposed to storytelling. Phenomenology's look of wonder, suggests Sarah Ahmed, does not have to occlude history, but may allow that history to come newly alive. "To re-encounter objects as strange things, "she writes, "is hence not to lose sight of their history but to refuse to make them history by losing sight."³¹ A gift of poetry is its single-minded attention to the sheer thingness of the thing, which may paradoxically reanimate and revitalize it, saving it from the abyss of oblivion or obsolescence.

In the mock solemnity of his hymn to "prodigious scissors," for example, Neruda pays tribute to a ubiquitous instrument, drawing attention to a beauty that inheres in function rather than being opposed to it. His quizzical look brings out the strange two-in-one-ness of scissors, "two long and treacherous / knives / crossed and bound together / for all time / two / tiny rivers / joined." These shiny strips of metal metamorphose under our gaze into quicksilver creatures, a "fish that swims across billowing linens / a bird / that flies / through barbershops." Agile and mobile, dexterous and fast-moving, "scissors / have gone / everywhere / they've explored / the world." Entangled in human lives, companionable if calmly indifferent, such daily things serve as precious repositories of associations and memories, marked with the traces and smells of their users, bearing witness to an infinity of accumulated acts and untold histories. Scissors have cut their way through history, trimming nails, making flags, chopping off hair, cutting out cancers; they are tangled up in the milestones of human existence, "cutting for newlyweds and the dead / for newborns and hospital wards." A mundane object turns out, on closer inspection, to be monumental in its sheer ubiquity, as indispensable as eyes or teeth, an astonishing prosthesis caught up in the endless symbolic and practical work of culture.³²

Such artfully simple poems about soap and scissors make a decisive break from an earlier body of work that was often, as in Neruda's Residence poems, soaked through with nightmarish visions of existential anguish and despair. The elemental odes marked a turn away from the modernist motif of the abject object; they are a world away from the malevolent matter that drags the narrator of *Nausea* to the edge of the abyss. Things in modernity are often recruited to serve as sources of melancholia or downright dread, epitomizing the opacity of the material world, its sullen recalcitrance or mulish resistance to our conceptual schemes. Neruda's things, by contrast, are neither spiky nor threatening, more inclined to nestle rather than bristle, making their homes among us like slightly eccentric pets or a sociable alien species. The elemental odes avoid the modern tendency to bifurcate objects into Gods or goods, in Douglas Mao's words, to press them into service as numinous reminders of some long-lost plenitude or retrograde indices of commercial culture.[33] Rather, we are invited to ponder the value of things in their muddied and mundane state, as they carry out their indispensable tasks, neither human nor inhuman but caught up in deeply symbiotic and sociable relations with their owners, our dogged companions from cradle to grave. Neruda's odes – a notable success with both critics and ordinary readers – do not anguish over the sheer impossibility of knowing the thing itself, but parse out a phenomenology of things as they appear to us, objects in everyday use, both utterly familiar yet newly mysterious in their rediscovered proximity and presence.

Such a phenomenological slant allows poetic description to circumvent the schism of subject and object that fuels traditional epistemologies, to elicit and to expand on our involvement in the world. We rediscover things as we know them to be, yet reordered and redescribed, shimmering in a transformed light.[34] Here again, we can see how the act of configuring draws on a repertoire of formal devices, understood not as intrinsic properties of literariness, but a flexible range of permutations and possibilities. Neruda strips words down to their bare bones, reducing them to sparse handfuls of nouns and commonplace adjectives; the abbreviated, fragmented, choppy lines, often a mere word or two long, are snipped short, as if by the scissors of which they speak. Such concision underscores the boundedness and finitude of the object; like the things they describe, Neruda's odes are handy and portable, they "fit in your pocket / smoothed and folded / like / a pair / of scissors." With a remarkable economy of scale, they rough out the qualities of onions and socks, form corresponding to function. To really see a thing, it turns out, may require an absence rather than an abundance of words; a few salient details, artfully ordered, rather than an exhaustive summation or encyclopedic description. Through their exemplary terseness, such poems remind us that knowing is shaped as much by what is left out as by what is kept in.

Abbreviation and incompleteness, we might conclude, haunt all of our efforts as writers or critics. Rather than estimating the falsehoods of literature from the secure standpoint of theory, we are called on to sort through the claims to persuasiveness, plausibility, and coherence of a multiplicity of genres. Each of these genres, whether fictional or factual, poetic or theoretical, creates a range of schemata, selects, organizes, and shapes language according to given criteria, opens up certain ways of seeing and closes off others. Each is composed of varying parts of blindness and insight, a condition as endemic to the theoretical text as the imaginative one. Before trying to remove the splinter from our neighbor's eye, in other words, we would do well to attend to the mote in our own.

That we access differing worlds through alternate frames of reference does not mean that we surrender all criteria of criticism and judgment, nor that such worlds are entirely alien or incommensurable. However, any clear-cut distinction between subjective and objective knowledge, ideology and science, literature and theory, falls apart. The work of art can no longer be barred from contributing to knowledge or advancing understanding.[35] Returning to Eagleton's *Criticism and Ideology*, for example, I am newly struck by its tortured equivocations, as the works of Austen and Dickens are deemed to offer a "sort of historical knowledge," "an analogue of knowledge," or "something approximating to knowledge." Back in 1976 Eagleton, like many other Marxist critics, cannot quite bring himself to endorse literature as a genuine form of knowledge, even though he admits that it is only because Austen's novels are *not* works of historical materialism that they can dwell on the details of "ethical discourse, rhetoric of character, ritual of relationship or ceremony of convention" that he finds so illuminating.[36]

Viewing literary texts as potential sources of insight does not mean that they cannot also mislead or mystify: as worldly objects, their mechanisms of sense-making remain fallible, not flawless. The salient point is that literature, by dint of its generic status as imaginative or fictional writing, cannot be automatically precluded from taking part in practices of knowing. The truths that literary texts harbor come, to be sure, in many different guises. In this chapter, I have focused on literature as a form of social knowledge, suggesting that such a coupling does not deserve to be seen as incongruous or oxymoronic. The worldly insights we glean from literary texts are not derivative or tautological, not stale, second-hand scraps of history or anthropology, but depend on a distinctive repertoire of techniques, conventions, and aesthetic possibilities. Through their rendering of the subtleties of social interaction, their mimicry of linguistic idioms and cultural grammars, their unblinking attention to the materiality of things, texts draw us into imagined yet referentially salient worlds. They do not just represent, but make newly present, significant shapes of social meaning; they crystallize, not just in what they show but in their address to the reader, what Merleau-Ponty calls the essential interwovenness of our being in the world. Their fictional and aesthetic dimensions, far from testifying to a failure of knowing, should be hailed as the source of their cognitive strength.

# 4

# *Shock*

Shock is symbolically central to contemporary literary studies, yet the word is not widely used, compared to its ubiquitous presence in art theory and cultural criticism. Does it seem too juvenile or low-brow, too redolent of multiple-car wrecks, teenage horror movies, or ageing punk-rockers? Perhaps its sheer viscerality jars with a sense of the mediated nature of literary response. Critics tiptoe around the subject of shock, preferring to approach it in oblique or circumspect fashion. When broaching the subject of literature's power to disturb, they are often drawn to a more specialized language of transgression, trauma, defamiliarization, dislocation, self-shattering, the sublime. While such terms have their uses, they are often driven by overdetermined agendas and weighed down with an excess of theoretical baggage. A word drawn from everyday usage can clear away some of our calcified and often under-justified convictions about the import and impact of literary works.

Shock, then, names a reaction to what is startling, painful, even horrifying. Applied to literary texts, it connotes something more brusque and brutal than, for example, the idea of *Stoss* advanced by Heidegger: the claim that what defines an artwork is its blow to consciousness, its rupturing of familiar frames of reference.[1] In the terms to be canvassed here, shocking is a selective epithet rather than a general synonym for aesthetic estrangement, patently more suited to some texts than others. My argument may resonate with modernists more than Victorianists, though modern art is by no means the only art to disturb and perturb. To be sure, ranking texts only in terms of their shock-value would result in an absurdly partial and eccentric list. Yet in my own history of reading – and I am hardly unique – the art of violence and violation has loomed disproportionately large.

I think back to my first encounter with the *Marat/Sade*. Peter Weiss's play within a play shows the Marquis de Sade directing a drama about the French revolution at the insane asylum at Charenton where he was long incarcerated. While Jean-Paul Marat, played by one of the inmates, sits in his bathtub awaiting his assassination by Charlotte Corday, he engages in spirited debate with de Sade about the meaning and purpose of revolution. These philosophical arguments, which pit Marx against Freud, Jacobin revolutionary fervor against an uncompromising insistence on human irrationality, are interspersed with scenes in which a motley caste of twitching and convulsive patients, erotomaniacs, somnabulists and ranting men in straitjackets, reenact key moments in the bloody history of the revolution. Finally, all pretense of belief in the therapeutic power of art comes to an end as the inmates of the asylum rise up in a frenzied, chaotic surge of revolt. Screaming "Revolution, revolution, copulation, copulation," they are brutally struck down by their attendants as de Sade looks on in world-weary amusement.

Other titles jostling for space on my undergraduate reading list were, it turned out, equally startling. Opening *Endgame* meant entering into a post-apocalyptic nightmare, a claustrophobic world stripped bare of sense and words where legless parents are stuffed into trash cans. In Bertolt Brecht's *The Measures Taken*, a band of revolutionary agitators calmly discuss whether to shoot one of their group whose spontaneous acts of kindness are damaging their cause; the play ends with a dispassionate description of him being executed and thrown into a pit. To open the pages of *Nausea* is to be met by a rancorous, misanthropic narrator who spews venom at the world and who is transfixed by the unmitigated horror of existence, by the sheer repulsiveness of the seething, fecund mass of being.

Encountering such texts felt like a slap in the face; an exhilarating assault equal parts intellectual and visceral. Here, indisputably, was the literature of extremity, of what Foucault and others call "the limit experience," a bracing blend of solipsism, paranoia, brutality, and despair, where the standard supports and consolations of every-day life are ruthlessly ripped away. Thanks to this early reading list, the metaphor of books as friends proposed by Wayne Booth and Martha Nussbaum has always struck me as counter-intuitive; books had many remarkable qualities, but they were certainly not friendly. Lionel Trilling's thesis made more sense: modern literature was the literature of violence and vituperation, derangement and destruction, an all-out, uncompromising attack on the foundations of culture.[2]

Trilling's essay was written over forty years ago, at a time when a proposal to teach a course on modernism could still raise eyebrows in the Columbia English department. Nowadays, it is often felt that we live in very different times, such that the association of literature with shock no longer holds. Here, for example, is Fredric Jameson, in his well-known account of postmodernism. "Not only are Joyce and Picasso no longer weird and repulsive, they have become classics and now look rather realistic to us. Meanwhile, there is very little in either the form or the content of contemporary art that contemporary society finds intolerable and scandalous."[3] Jameson juxtaposes the explosive impact of modernism, the sheer outrageousness of its original assault on social taboos and conventions, to our own blunted sensibility. We are now immune to the shocking insofar shock itself has become routine; we inhabit a world of frenetic change and frantic rhythms, immersed in a culture that is driven by an insatiable demand for novelty and sensation. If the aura of revolution is now a styling and marketing advantage, if transgression is harnessed to the selling of sneakers and a cornucopia of sexual perversions is only a mouse-click away, then surely the project of the avant-garde is irrevocably exhausted. Under such conditions, shock is irrevocably stripped of any remaining shred of authenticity.

Jameson's thesis radiates a seductive air of finality, while suffer-ing the flaws of a strong historicism that seeks to conjure epochal totalities out of evidentiary fragments. There is something far too schematic about such efforts to shoe-horn the vagaries of affective and aesthetic response into an orderly sequence of historical stages. No one would dispute that we no longer inhabit the world of the

Victorians or early moderns, that we cannot recapture the sheer outrage or astonishment felt by those confronted, for the very first time, with the alien daubs of Picasso or the aphasic stutterings of Stein. We can concur that contemporary culture is more attuned to the lure of the perverse and the bizarre, that our world is notably less staid than that of our forebears. But does it really follow that literature has been stripped of all capacity to shock, that it has been irrevocably defanged by the onward march of history? Can works of art no longer punch us in the gut?

Let me offer up a few of my own evidentiary fragments. Most of my undergraduate students seemed just as nonplussed by *Nausea* in 2004 as I was three decades earlier. Reading Witold Gombrowicz's remarkable *Pornografia* and Yukio Mishima's *The Sailor Who Fell From Grace With the Sea* several years ago left distinct sensations of queasiness in my stomach. While researching a book on tragic women, I regularly encounter the testimony of critics who reach for epithets such as "harrowing," "hellish," and "horrifying" to describe performances of ancient and contemporary tragedies. Are all these reactions self-deluded? (And what exactly would it be mean to be mistaken about one's own sense of shock?) Or do we need to rethink our ideas of shock, and to wrench them away, at least in part, from the tradition of the avant-garde?

To ponder this tradition is to view a motley assortment of movements – dada, Surrealism, Futurism and the like – frenetically debunking mythologies and slaughtering all sacred cows except one: the authenticity of their own antinomian stance. Pulling the rug out from under bourgeois complacency, spitting in the face of the powers-that-be, the avant-garde calls for modes of engagement that are excessive, visceral, over the top, in-your-face. Provocation, extremity, defiance, revolt are its buzzwords and by-words; there is an irresistible pull to the purity of violent action, a call for brass knuckles to bash in the world's skull. Its aesthetic is modeled on the shout, the electric shock, the wailing scream of sirens on city streets. Avant-garde manifestos demand the destruction of museums, libraries, academies of every kind, urge the death of the bourgeois family, delight in the destruction of property, prophesy the annihilation of logic, reason and all systems. "We are like a raging wind," declares Tzara in his dada manifesto, "we are preparing the great spectacle of disaster, conflagration and decomposition."[4]

If we take such declarations too literally, no doubt, we miss the elements of sheer bravado and theatricality in the manifesto form. Yet critics often wax disconsolate, if not despairing, when contrasting such soaring ambitions to the subsequent fate of the avant-garde. That which disdains all compromise is sucked into the mainstream; a defiant and deviant anti-art is welcomed into the museum; the flame of revolutionary fervor is snuffed out by institutional acceptance. Rather than striking fear into the hearts of bourgeois bankers, avant-garde art turns out to be an attractive accouterment, even a sought-after investment. Yet such an anti-climactic ending was hardly unexpected; the avant-garde ultimately underwrote rather than rejected the modern religion of art, endowing its own project with a furious, cleansing, annihilating power that it could not possibly sustain. It is the fate of all iconoclasms, Jean-Joseph Goux dryly notes, to keep alive the very myths that they hope to destroy.[5] How could manifestos, poems, or ready-mades topple the walls of institutions or bring alienation to an end in one stroke? In the very vehemence and absoluteness of its acts of negation, the avant-garde clung to an extraordinarily utopian aesthetics and politics.

Before concluding that shock has been rendered obsolete, we would do well to peel it away from such a history of over-heated oratory and inflated claims. Conflating revolution in art with revolution in life is a peculiarly modern mistake, guaranteed to inspire absurdly high hopes of the transformative energies of texts. That works of art cannot topple banks and bureaucracies, museums and markets, does not mean, according to the theoretical back-flip demanded by an absolutist logic, that they are therefore doomed to be impotent and inert, stripped of all power to challenge perception or shake up the psyche. We do such works a patent injustice by forcing them into prefabricated slots of revolution or cooption, transgression or containment, overlooking the possibility of more muted or qualified transformations. Indeed, while the star of the avant-garde has indisputably waned, a vanguardist belief in the emancipatory power of shock still flourishes in literary theory. We are currently in the midst of what can only be called a glamorizing of transgression, as literary critics bolster their radical credentials by expanding on ever more outré topics from sex toys to serial killers.

Such a cult of outsiderdom, however, sanitizes an aesthetic of shock by glossing over its authentically disturbing elements; it looks over, rather than into, the abyss. The Romantic yearning for an escape from social constraints crops up whenever critics speak of transgression and freedom in the same breath, as if the proliferation of shock, horror, and disgust will somehow, of their own volition, usher in a longed for liberation or a democratic utopia. Even a cursory familiarity with the work of de Sade or Bataille should be enough to expose the folly of such a belief. The literature of shock becomes truly disquieting not when it is shown to further social progress, but when it utterly fails to do so, when it slips through our frameworks of legitimation and resists our most heartfelt values. It is at that point that we are left floundering and speechless, casting about for words to make sense of our own response.

The ethos of the avant-garde claims shock as its ultimate weapon, a strategy for confounding and astounding the dim-witted bourgeoisie, the credulous masses, the pompous prelates and guardians of culture. A clear line is drawn between insiders and outsiders, the insolent insurgents and the sadly unenlightened, those who shock and the hypocrites and charlatans who deserve to be shocked. Shock is seized as a source of symbolic advantage, a guarantee of oppositional purity or redemptive politics, shoring up the certitude of one's own advanced consciousness. It is, in short, eviscerated of any genuine terror. Yet it is also possible for shock to work in other ways: to blur the distinction between self and other, to unravel the certainty of one's own convictions rather than sustaining them. Shock in this sense is not a blithe herald of future freedom from all tyrannies and oppressions but a graphic illustration of the internal as well as external obstacles that lie in the way of such freedom.

*The Bacchae* is often held up as one of the most shocking Greek tragedies, a far from paltry achievement in a corpus of plays replete with incest, suicide, adultery, parricide, matricide, mass slaughter, and unspeakable atrocities of various kinds. The young ruler Pentheus, eager to stamp out the cult of Dionysus that is taking root in Thebes, intends to bring an army against the maenads worshipping on the mountainside. A mysterious stranger, the god himself in disguise, persuades him to first observe their sacred rituals, convincing Pentheus to put on women's clothes so that he will not be recognized as an intruder. Yet Agave, Pentheus' mother and one of the worshippers, her wits beclouded by Dionysus, mistakes her son for a mountain lion and tears him limb from limb in a frenzy of blood lust. "Ignoring his cries of pity," the text tells us, "she seized his left arm at the wrist; then, planting / her foot upon his chest, she pulled, wrenching away / the arm at the shoulder – not by her own strength / for the god had put inhuman power in her hands."[6] Her fellow worshippers break off pieces of his flesh, one woman grabbing a forearm, another seizing hold of a foot; they toss the meat to each other, we are told, like balls in a game of catch. Only as Agave bears the lion's head proudly onto the stage, does the truth slowly dawn upon her: that the body she has torn apart with such frenzied abandon is the one to which she gave birth.

What exactly is it about *The Bacchae* that renders it so shocking? Partly, no doubt, the sheer gruesomeness of its subject matter; even in our own jaded times, descriptions of women tossing chunks of human flesh to each other and ripping their children to shreds are far from routine. This dissolution of boundaries brings not freedom but homicidal madness and terror in its wake. While a feminist reading would note the association of femininity with otherness, frenzy and bestiality, the play also rips apart the very distinctions – of male/female, human/animal, reason/madness – that it engages. Pentheus, anxious to assert his manly control over the maenads on the mountainside, turns into the hapless plaything of the god that he abhors. His urge to impose rationality and the order of the polis only underscores his own crazed obsessiveness; his dislike of women results in his own adoption of women's dress; his loathing of Dionysus brings out the Dionysian depths of his own personality, in a twist that the authors of the *Dialectic of Enlightenment* would approve. Moreover, even as *The Bacchae* underscores the grisly horror of Pentheus' death, it offers no standpoint from which such horror can be condemned as aberrant or exceptional. From the words of the chorus, made up of barbarian female worshippers of Dionysus, to the final appearance of the god himself, serenely indifferent to the human wreckage and suffering he has caused, the play offers us no clear ethical foothold, no means to pass judgment – scholars have wrangled endlessly over whether *The Bacchae* is a celebration or a critique of Dionysian cults. The "sparagmos" that the play acts out for us – the dismembering and scattering of the human body – is also a ruthless rending of the frameworks through which we might make sense of such actions.

As the ultimate Dionysian drama, *The Bacchae* appears to leave little room for a redemptive or reconciliatory reading; for the once widely touted idea that tragedy, by bestowing order and intelligibility on terrible events, distances us from the experience of suffering. Jean-Pierre Vernant restates the case in the following words:

> Because the subject dramatized by the tragedy is a fiction, the effect produced by the painful or terrifying events that it presents on stage is quite different from what it would be if those events were real. They touch and concern us, but only from a distance. They are happening somewhere else, not in real life. Because they only exist on an imaginary level, they are set at a distance even as they are represented. Their effect upon the public, which remains uninvolved, is to "purify" the feelings of fear and pity that they would arouse in real life.[7]

Such an appraisal is hard-pressed to account for the visceral, affective, gut-wrenching impact of works such as *The Bacchae* (the idea of catharsis, we might remember, was originally associated with the eminently physical activity of purging one's bowels). The widespread belief that tragic emotions are restricted to pity and fear, moreover, leaves no room for reflecting on the shudder of shock triggered by some, if not all, tragic art.

Shock builds on a sense of fear, serving as a synonym for terror or intense fright, while also shading towards rather different associations of disgust and repulsion. If we find ourselves shocked by graphic portrayals of organs or orifices, secretions or excretions, our reaction does not spring from any real or imagined threat to our safety; the affront is to our moral or aesthetic sensibilities rather than our physical well-being. Alternatively, shock may trigger a notable absence of emotion, conjuring up a state of numbness or blankness much canvassed by trauma theorists. Shock, then, tells us less about the specific content of an affective state than about the qualitative impact of a text or object on the psyche. It denotes a sudden collision, an abrupt, even violent, encounter; the essence of shock is to be jarring. Unlike pity and fear, it is fueled by an essential element of surprise; while we can fear what we already know, shock presumes an encounter with the unexpected, an experience of being wrenched in an altered frame of mind. Even if we anticipate what is to come, as in the dramatization of a familiar myth, we still find ourselves smacking up against the unimaginable, the dreaded and dreadful, the too-horrible-for-words. Shock pivots around the quality of what Karl Heinz Bohrer calls "suddenness," a violent rupture of continuity and coherence, as time is definitively and dramatically rent asunder into a "before" and "after." It displays a distinctive temporality characterized by a logic of punctuation, as the continuum of experience shatters into disconnected segments marked by dramatic variations of intensity.[8]

Shock thus marks the antithesis of the blissful enfolding and voluptuous pleasure that we associate with enchantment. Instead of being rocked and cradled, we find ourselves ambushed and under assault; shock invades consciousness and broaches the reader's or viewer's defenses. Smashing into the psyche like a blunt instrument, it can wreak havoc on our usual ways of ordering and understanding the world. Our sense of equilibrium is destroyed; we are left at sea, dazed and confused, fumbling for words, unable to piece together a coherent response. Woven out of variegated strands of revulsion, horror, and disbelief, shock can temporarily disable both mind and body. And while its immediate effects may quickly dissipate, the after-shocks can reverberate in the psyche for some time; the suddenness of the initial impact is succeeded by an extended, delayed, or belated array of psychic or somatic reactions.

*Contra* Vernant, I would also venture that the correlation between art's unreality and the intensity of its emotional impact is far from clear-cut. No one would dispute that our sense of anguish at the suffering of a person close to us far exceeds, in its intensity and magnitude, our response to a work of art. By the same token, however, we may be more deeply shaken and unnerved by a gut-wrenching Sarah Kane play than by any number of death statistics reported in the newspaper. Works of art can bring home, with exceptional vividness and graphic power, psychic dramas of torment and self-loathing, destructiveness and disgust, even as they zoom in unsparingly on flayed bodies, staring eye-sockets, or obscenely gaping wounds. Rather than serving up suffering at a distance, they allow us to witness it close up, magnified to the nth degree, sometimes in lurid and blood-spattered detail. What they lack in factual truth they more than make up for in emotional force. The belief that we gauge artworks at arm's length, shrouded in a protective blanket of aesthetic disinterest, reveals more about the critical doxa of a particular moment than about the psychic realities of aesthetic response.

Moreover, works such as *The Bacchae* call on us to reassess our ingrained beliefs about the temporality of shock. According to an avant-garde logic that still haunts our thinking, tradition is the ultimate enemy, an archetype of paternal authority that must be overthrown and slain in order to make way for the radically new and not-yet. How, then, do we explain that works from the distant past can be more disquieting and disturbing than those of the present? Why do texts that are venerated, widely analyzed, and indisputably canonized pack a more powerful emotional punch than their successors? How do we account for the shock of the old? Rather than subsuming a shock aesthetic within a storyline of linear development, we can seize on shock, in a Benjaminian spirit, to crack open conventional models of history.

Modern criticism deems novelty to be an essential source of aesthetic surprise, assuming that shock is tied to a single moment of impact. When a new form or genre appears on the scene, its effect is to render the ordinary strange, to challenge our usual ways of seeing, to startle us out of the torpor of habitual perceptions and received ideas. In altering how we see, it also changes what we see. Yet this effect, by its very nature, can only be finite and short-lived. Shock is gradually drained of its emotive impact and power to change consciousness. Disorientation gives way to eventual acceptance as once puzzling or bizarre forms of expression are gradually absorbed into our cultural lexicon. The history of literature is thus driven by an endless spiral of surprise-habituation-surprise, as established styles yield to new techniques that can again revitalize perception.

This argument, most doggedly pursued within Russian formalism, makes intuitive sense as a way of grasping the logic of aesthetic change in the modern West. And yet it also oversimplifies and underestimates the impact of literary works by yoking them too emphatically to a single moment. Art, in this view, can only surprise us for an instant, is subsequently eviscerated of all power to change consciousness and provoke thought, is rendered flat, stale, and humdrum by the passing of time. This is the mindset of what Wai Chee Dimock calls synchronic historicism: the belief that a work's resonance is entirely contained within one slice of time, usually the period of its first appearance.[9] Literary meaning, however, does not reveal itself in a flash, and texts do not disclose themselves irrevocably and absolutely at the moment of their first appearance. What of their potential to resonate across time and the power of past art to disorient or disturb? We might think of such texts as time travelers or even time bombs, incendiary devices packed with an explosive force that unleashes itself long after the moment of their manufacture. Our ideas about the aesthetics of shock are hampered by a sequential and progressive view of history, overly constrained by a mindset that conceives of the shocking as synonymous with the new.

*Penthesilea* was written in 1808: triggering expressions of revulsion among its early critics, it was accused of showcasing frenzied abnormalities and hideous perversions. Yet it would be hard to conclude that we are now impervious to those elements that inspired sputters of outrage on its first appearance. Kleist's drama stages a sex war, a clash of obsessions, a frenzied, foaming-at-the-mouth fight to the death between Achilles and Penthesilea, queen of the Amazons. The Amazonian ruler, struck with an intemperate passion for

Achilles, must court him with her sword; Amazonian law decrees that its citizens engage in sexual congress only with men captured in the heat of battle. Achilles, equally infatuated by the warrior princess, triumphs in one of their violent skirmishes, yet chooses to conceal his victory, pretending that he is her prisoner rather than she his. Enraged and humiliated when she discovers the truth, Penthesilea once more charges furiously into battle. In this final encounter, Achilles comes toward her unarmed and defenseless, all too happy to humor the beautiful Amazon by miming surrender for the sake of the sexual pleasure that awaits him.

Yet what is for Achilles a playful game of erotic conquest is for the warrior princess in deadly earnest. Oscillating in intensifying confusion between an ideal of female self-governance grounded in a warrior code of honor and the equally insistent pull of an erotic script that calls for female submission, Penthesilea is driven into madness. Her final response to this double bind is to drive an arrow through Achilles' throat and then to throw herself at his wounded body in a fit of delirium, ripping his flesh apart with her teeth in the company of her hounds. "She sinks – tearing the armor off his body – / Into his ivory breast she sinks her teeth, / She and her savage dogs in competition, / Oxus and Sphinx chewing into his right breast, / And she into his left; when I arrived, / The blood was dripping from her mouth and hands."[10]

Much of the commentary on *Penthesilea* has centered on its metafictional features, reading the play as an allegory of the antinomies and pitfalls of language. Critics show how linguistic confusion, double meanings, the blurring of the metaphorical and the literal, are deeply woven into this drama of culture clash and gender war. In its most famous passage, as Penthesilea comes to realize the horror of her cannibalistic slaying, she admits to an all too unfortunate "slip of the tongue," a confusion of signifiers (*küssen/bissen*; kiss/bite) that are all too easily mistaken. Her actions, she suggests in a dazed monologue, are simply the literalizing of an all too common metaphor: "How many a maid will say, her arms wrapped round / her lover's neck: I love you, oh so much / That if I could, I'd eat you up right here."[11] This is a play where the sexual and the textual are persistently interfused. Yet there is also something oddly incongruous about these efforts to frame Kleist's play as a meditation on linguistic undecidability or the relative merits of metaphor versus simile. Critics seem compelled to highlight the scholarly sophistication of their own readings by averting their eyes from anything as crass as the carnage of the play's content.

Michel Chaouli is on to something when he juxtaposes *Penthesilea* to the *Critique of Judgment* and argues that Kleist's drama is perturbing because it violates the prohibition against representations of the disgusting. While ugliness is permissible in art, the disgusting is not, according to Kant, because it forces itself upon us as a visceral response beyond our control. Moreover, Kant is bent on drawing a clear line between the reflective exercise of aesthetic taste and the crude sensory stimulation of physical taste. *Penthesilea* makes mayhem of this distinction as its heroine, characterized from the start by the voracity of her cravings, seeks to gobble up the distance between herself and Achilles. Shown at the start as a resplendent, aesthetic object, radiant and shining like the sun, Achilles is all too soon transformed into nothing more than a dead lump of meat, "reversing the metaphorization of taste, accrued over several centuries, in a matter of a few hours."[12] In tracing a narrative arc from the beautiful to the disgusting, *Penthesilea* blurs the line between taste as reflective aesthetic judgment and taste as animalistic appetite and cannibalistic craving.

Such observations speak to a somatic register of response that receives short shrift in literary criticism, yet that cannot help but intrude into any discussion of shock. Art that disturbs or appalls can trigger a spectrum of physical reactions: a sudden gag in the throat; unbidden, unwanted tears; an involuntary flinching away from a too-graphic image; a sudden crop of goose bumps or chills on the skin; gusts of nervous laughter erupting in a darkened auditorium. We are rudely ripped from aesthetic reflection to the baseline workings of biology, confronted with the stark evidence of our involuntary responses: the manufacturing of adrenalin, the acceleration of heart rate, the constriction of blood vessels. Our body may react even before our mind registers what it is at stake, underscoring the extent of our emotional suggestibility and physical vulnerability. Images and words inscribe their all too material effects on our bodies from a distance, as if through a mysterious machinery of remote control; we feel ourselves stirred by forces we only vaguely apprehend. The protective shield of the psyche is broached; our sense of autonomy and separateness is bruised; we are no longer in full command of our own response. We find ourselves in the realm of the abject, floored by the sheer physicality of our reactions, newly conscious of being stranded on the perilous border of nature and culture.

At this point, Leo Bersani's idiom of self-shattering cannot help but come to mind. Taking up a psychoanalytic perspective at odds with Jameson's historicism, Bersani insists on the fundamental contemporaneity of shock, as a form of psychic disruption impervious to chronological markers. Human sexuality, according to Bersani, is grounded in masochism, making us ontologically implicated in violence from our earliest years. "Our choice is not between violence and nonviolence," he declares, "but is rather between the psychic dislocations of mobile desire and a destructive fixation on anecdotal violence."[13] While critical of realism's attempts to master the workings of desire through narrative and anecdote, Bersani lauds the writing of Baudelaire, Genet, and others for undermining all pretence of coherence by violating the structures of the self. Such an aesthetic of dissolution, he proposes, liberates us from totalitarian models of identity and the sheer implausibility of our notions of individuality.

Bersani is surely right to highlight the masochistic thrill of aesthetic shock, the painful pleasure caused by a temporary release from the prison-house of the self and its retinue of burdens and obligations. Yet a psychoanalytical framework cannot account for the variable connotations of shock, nor the reasons why it surges to prominence in some periods of creativity and not in others. Indeed, Bersani's insistence on the radically asocial and disruptive aspects of shock seems at odds with his own evident success in making a career out of writing about it, even as the rhetoric of self-shattering risks hyperbole – while consciousness can be modified by reading, it is far from destroyed or definitively dispersed. Without launching into yet

118

another adjudication between Freud and Foucault, we can surmise that shock speaks to both social and asocial aspects of human existence, that it can bring us face to face with what is deeply unnerving, terrifying, or taboo, but that it is also a cultural signifier drafted into service to connote Romantic bravado, counter-cultural authenticity, or intellectual prestige.

In any event, a Freudian etiology risks defusing and diluting an aesthetic of shock by slotting it into a predetermined explanatory frame. I am more interested in the challenge that psychoanalysis poses to a progressive and linear model of time, as a backward-facing philosophy that envisions the self as eternally suspended within the sticky threads of its own history. Far from being a record of superseded errors and obsolete traditions to be heedlessly abandoned as we forge into the future, the past serves as a graphic reminder of the tortuous path of our own becoming, of the many ways in which the "before" continues to bear down on and mold the "after." Such a train of thought leads beyond the psyche to open up larger questions of textual temporality, of how works resonate beyond the confines of a single historical moment.

It is surprising, in this regard, that *Nachträglichkeit* has not broken out of its psychoanalytical niche to play a more central and commanding role in literary theory. Most successfully translated as "afterwardness," it crystallizes the idea that meaning is not embedded once and for all in a particular moment, but diffused across a temporal continuum. In its therapeutic sense, the term names a traumatic event that is registered at a later date when the individual belatedly grasps its import, with the *locus classicus* being Freud's study of the Wolf Man. Thanks to this time-lag between the occurrence of an event and its resonance, meaning is delayed, washed forward into the future rather than anchored in one defining moment. And even as fragments of past experience persist into the present, their meaning mutates under the pressure of new insight. Retrospection recreates the past even as it retrieves it, in a mutual contamination and commingling of different times.[14]

This insight speaks directly to the enigmas of textual transmission: how do we hold fast to the idea that works bear the imprint of their historical moment, while also accounting for their potential to resonate across time? Our temporal frameworks are notably more impoverished than our schema for conceptualizing space. Post-colonial studies has issued a vigorous challenge to spatially segregated models of national and ethnic identity by introducing the language of hybridity, translation, and global flow. Analogous models are sorely needed for conceptualizing the cross-temporal movement or migration of texts. Historical criticism enriches our understanding of the provenance of a work of art, but it can also inspire a stunted view of texts as governed entirely by the conditions of their origin, leaving us hard-pressed to explain the continuing timeliness of texts, their potential ability to speak across centuries.

The idea of "afterwardness" speaks to this delayed or belated transmission, highlighting the transtemporal movements of texts and their unpredictable dynamics of address. Rather than lapsing into a dormant or moribund state after a founding flash of glory, works of art may experience a hectic, even frenetic, afterlife characterized by new convergences and mutating constellations of meaning. Circumventing any desire on our part to relegate them to a hinter-land of outdated or regressive beliefs, texts from the past can inter-rupt our stories of cultural progress, speak across centuries, spark moments of affinity across the gulf of temporal difference. Their very untimeliness renders them newly timely. As Benjamin puts it in his famous discussion of the dialectical image: "the Then and the Now come together into a constellation like a flash of lightning."[15] Rather than being sequestered in a remote historical preserve, what is old can smash into the present and affect perception in the now. An aesthetics of shock, rather than being yoked to newness and up-to-dateness, turns out to be driven by a much more variable and volatile temporality.

Yet even as shock can shake up the complacency of what Elisabeth Ladenson aptly calls chronological chauvinism, it also yields to the pressures of history; that readers of different periods may be shocked by the same works does not mean that they are shocked in the same way.[16] Indeed, the idea of shock acquires a distinctively new sheen and substance in modernity as a response to deep-seated changes in the textures and rhythms of human experience. Georg Simmel famously expounds on this question, arguing that the modern sensibility is driven by a craving for excitement, a yearning for extreme impressions. The desire to shock and be shocked acquires an unprecedented intensity and visibility in the fabric of modern life, displayed in the sensational thrills and spills of cinema and other popular entertainments as well as the calculated outrages of the avant-garde. To be modern, it seems, is to be addicted to surprise and speed, to jolts of adrenalin and temporal rupture: to be a shockaholic.

Yet the reasons put forward to explain this shift in taste and temperament are notably at odds. Shock effects, it is claimed, are woven deep into the fabric of modernity, thanks to the chaotic range of stimuli, the bustle and jostling confusion of the crowd, the hectic barrage of information and audiovisual disarray that make up the experience of urban living. The human sensorium, responding to the swiftly changing milieu of the city, becomes newly adapted and even addicted to suddenness, eagerly pursuing sensations of novelty, thrills of excitement, jolts, unexpected transitions. Aesthetic shock, in this reading, is continuous with modernity. But the attraction of shock is also attributed to a blanketing sense of boredom, whether the grinding monotony of the production line or the studied melancholy of a quasi-metaphysical malady. A felt dullness and deadening of emotion, along with the anesthetic, soul-destroying effects of modern routines, triggers a desire for extreme sensations and an addiction to the adrenalin rush of intense emotion. The sharp stab of pain, the electrifying jolt of disgust, offers a welcome release from the numbness of not being able to feel. Moreover, the manicured nature of modern life, with its sugar-coated reassurances and its sweeping of unpleasant truths under the carpet, calls forth a desire to go eyeball to eyeball with the squalid and unpalatable elements of human experience. Shock, in this view, is a reaction to modernity.

Both of these facets of modern consciousness – hypersensitivity and stagnation, stimulation and torpor – permeate the work of Baudelaire, the poet most closely identified with an aesthetic of shock, thanks to Walter Benjamin's influential commentary. How, asks Benjamin, does lyric poetry respond to a world in which shock experience has become the norm?[17] Baudelaire's work is hailed as a defensive response to modernity, a way of processing the histrionic jolts and shudders of modern urban experience by transforming them into poetic figures. Yet his poems do not just record shock, but also perpetuate it in their own performances, parrying jolts with jolts, meeting violence with counter-violence. Shock is both an adaptive defense to the swirling chaotic sensations of city life and a purposeful act of aggression on the part of the writer striking out at his public, fashioning a phenomenology of literary assault. The modern experience of discontinuity and suddenness, abruptness and surprise, is echoed in poetic forms that undercut the reader's certainties, court perversity, engage in discordant juxtapositions and poetic dissonance, plant punches and counter-punches.

Of course, many of the features that outraged Baudelaire's contemporaries now seem less than scandalous; whatever we think of his lesbian poems, for example, we are unlikely to find them shocking. The Romantic cult of Satanism, with its hookahs, vampires, and doom-laden invocations of the abyss, can seem quaintly superannuated, even as once daring breaches of diction and stylistic decorum no longer raise any eyebrows. The figure of the *poète maudit*, endlessly replicated in the annals of the contemporary art market as well as a stream of bad-boy rock stars, has long since edged into the realm of cliché. Yet certain poems of *Les Fleurs du Mal* still manage to pack a considerable punch. "La Charogne," or "A Carcass," for example, opens in unexceptional fashion, as the poet, speaking to his mistress, calls up the memory of a shared summer morning. Yet the conventional poetic address of *mon âme* (my soul) purposefully grates with the rhyming reference to the *charogne infâme* (vile carrion) that the couple once glimpsed lying by the roadside. The animal carcass, its legs thrown up in the air, its belly exposed, roasting in the sun, brings to the speaker's mind the picture of a woman burning in the throes of desire: the fervor of sexual abandon mimics and foreshadows the ultimate obscenity of death. Zeroing in remorselessly on signs of rottenness and decay, the poet does not just remind his lover of her recoil of revulsion, but forces her to relive the experience yet again, bringing past horrors to fresh life through the gloating and sadistic precision of his graphic descriptions: "la puanteur était si forte, que sur l'herbe / vous crûtes vous évanouir" (the stench was so strong that you thought you would faint on the grass).[18] There is a hallucinatory quality to the poem's invocation of unbearably intense sensations bearing in from all sides: the heat of the sun beating down; the putrid fumes emanating from the dead animal's stomach; the graphic image of the splayed carcass; the sounds of the flies buzzing around its rotting belly. This is nature imagined not as solace or refuge, but as a brutal attack on visual, olfactory, and auditory modes of perception, a vile synesthesia of the repellent and obscene.

Moreover, we are slowly made aware that the corpse is in a state of perpetual motion; maggots are pouring like a viscous liquid across the ragged remains of the body, falling and rising like a series of waves. The poet is struck by the sheer beauty of this rhythmic movement as it mimics the music of running water and the sound of the wind. Even as he conjures up the horror of death jerked back to life, of flesh uncannily animated by the worms that are consuming it, he wrenches us into an awareness of the remarkable symmetries that thrive in the midst of putrefaction. Yet this aestheticizing gaze does not annul the horror of what is being evoked but accentuates it; the rotting carcass is both like, yet utterly unlike, the blossoming flower to which it is compared. As in the famous duck/rabbit picture, we are unable to synthesize these competing mental images, but are forced to oscillate between disjunctive registers of revulsion and aesthetic pleasure, in the collision of incommensurables often noted as an element of Baudelairean style. The sheer gruesomeness of the poem's subject matter is accentuated by the final picture of a cur lurking in the shadows, waiting to snap its jaws around the rotting carcass and to perpetuate the cycle of ingestion and incorporation.

It is only under certain conditions, to be sure, that putrefaction can be mined for a frisson of shock; for much of human history, the sight of a rotting animal carcass would have been too humdrum to be worthy of attention. We are invited to imagine the poet's mistress as an over-refined Parisian coquette estranged from the rural rhythms of birth and death and burdened by a distinctively modern sense of fastidiousness and *pudeur*. Whatever the misogyny of the poem's guiding conceit – that the sex closest to the state of nature is also the sex most hypocritically squeamish about natural processes – it raises intriguing questions about the history of human shockability. Are we really less likely to find ourselves disgusted, horrified, or appalled than our predecessors, as Jameson claims? While in some areas we display a level of insouciance that is distinctively new, when it comes to sexual relations between adults and children, for example, our sense of moral outrage has clearly intensified. Moreover, as historians of the civilizing process like to point out, we have grown ever more sensitive to, and repulsed by, reminders of our mortality – disease, decay, suppurating wounds, rotting flesh, nauseating body odors and the like – even as once commonplace exchanges of bodily fluids – mothers breastfeeding other women's children, strangers drinking from the same cup – are now likely to inspire shivers of disgust. Rather than tracing out a single developmental arc from repression to enlightenment, from outrage to blasé indifference, the history of modernity involves an unmaking and remaking of prohibitions and taboos.

In juxtaposing the responses of the poet and his lover, Baudelaire's poem is structured around a symbolic bifurcation of shocker and shocked. An emotional division of labor is established, with the agitation and revulsion of his mistress serving as a foil for the poet's own imperturbable gaze. Her distress underscores his ability to soar beyond the sheer obviousness of disgust, to alchemize dross into gold and salvage traces of beauty from the ugly and the obscene. Rather than a collectively experienced ritual, as in *The Bacchae*, the aesthetics of shock now serves to mark boundaries and draw distinctions, allowing bohemian Paris to give voice to its anomic disdain for bourgeois and feminine sensibilities. The personal costs of sustaining such distinctions should not be underplayed – we need only think of Baudelaire's painful and poverty-stricken circumstances and his notorious battles with the censors. And yet, to romanticize shock

as absolutely transgressive is to overlook the ways in which it is subsequently folded into hierarchies of social distinction. The view that
repugnant, horrible, or distasteful objects are appropriate subjects
for art will have become, by the mid-twentieth century, a virtually
obligatory accouterment of upper-middle-class taste.[19] The aesthetics of shock will also accrue a certain amount of symbolic capital
by counterposing masculine bravado to feminine squeamishness and
over-refinement; "La Charogne" is far from the only modernist work
to ratify its own aesthetic violations as an assault on feminine
prudery. Literary provocation has historically been a male province,
even though it is women who are usually hauled in to symbolize
the miasmic terrors of unregulated desire and to embody the
elemental insight that we all, in William Miller's words, "generate,
fornicate, secrete, excrete, suppurate, die, and rot."[20]

Interestingly enough, however, there is a shadow history of shock
that is often overlooked by acolytes of transgression. *The Flowers of
Evil* coincided with a voluminous outpouring of lurid sensationalist
fiction across the Channel, coupled with copious commentary
about the perils of a literature that appeals directly to the senses and
bypasses rational reflection. Popular favorites such as *Mrs. Audley's
Secret, The Woman in White*, and *East Lynne* were hailed as deeply
harrowing, accused of jangling the nerves or over-stimulating the senses.
What defined the sensation novel was its power to excite and
agitate its readers; according to Margaret Oliphant, it "thrills us into
wonder, terror, and breathless interest, with positive personal shocks
of surprise and excitement."[21] Like earlier avatars such as the Gothic
novel, sensationalist fiction proved especially attractive to female
writers and readers, underscoring a culture-wide appetite for lurid
topics and jarring juxtapositions. Far from being tied to an avant-
garde and modernist trajectory, shock turns out to have much wider
resonance and appeal. That such fiction falls outside the radar of Bersani
and others has much to do, no doubt, with its overlaying of shock
with sentimentality, its managing of psychic disturbances via the coherence of well-ordered and morally driven plots. Yet any conclusion
that such fiction is therefore conscripted to cement normative
models of identity relies on an overly literal assessment that hews

125

too closely to the surface level of narrative and authorial commentary. Readers' fascination with taboo subjects and marginal figures may cut across, or undermine, such ordering devices, generating more visceral, inchoate, or unruly responses.

In the contemporary literary scene, moreover, any ingrained assumptions about the masculinity of shock are quickly turned on their head. We need only think of Kathy Acker, with her cartoonish sex parts, scatological vocabulary, and obsession with incest, or Elfriede Jelinek's pitiless tableaus of female sexual masochism, mother-daughter hatred, and mindless adolescent cruelty. In Helen Zahavi's exuberant, blood-spattered revenge fantasy, *Dirty Weekend*, the heroine gleefully massacres the various men who have pestered or molested her, while the afore-mentioned plays of Sarah Kane have been lauded and condemned for scenarios that test the limits of onstage performance, ranging from defecation to disemboweling to baby-eating. As a history of expectations about the nature of femininity comes under intense stress, ever more female writers are turning toward an aesthetic of provocation and perversity.[22]

A novel by Gayl Jones crystallizes how a seemingly asocial aesthetics of shock is scarred by the traces of race as well as sex. *Eva's Man* is a first-person narrative told by a black woman incarcerated for the murder of her lover. In laconic and often expressionless fashion, Eva speaks of meeting a man in a bar, going back with him to his hotel room, and finally poisoning him and perhaps (the details remain intentionally blurred) biting off his penis. Written in a spare and tightly scripted vernacular, this desolate account unfolds via an elaborate triadic temporal structure that shifts, from paragraph to paragraph and sometimes from sentence to sentence, between the narrative present of the jail cell, Eva's memories of her childhood, and an inconclusive account of the events leading up to the murder five years previously. Opening in relatively coherent fashion, it quickly unravels as the text splinters into a heap of historically disconnected yet symbolically connected fragments.

This temporal fluidity, however, is far from liberating, intensifying a relentless sense of claustrophobia, of unspeakable horrors closing in inexorably from all directions. Particular phrases are hammered home again and again, conveying a rhythm of eternal and unchanging sameness, of a destiny not to be avoided. "Act like a whore, I'll fuck you like a whore"; "you too old not to had the meat"; "once you open your legs, Miss Billie said, you caint close them." Jones crafts a nightmarish picture of being reduced to a sexual thing, of a world where nothing exists beyond the threat or reality of copulation. While such episodes appear to indict the sexual exploitation of girls and women, the antirealism of their collective impact – the fact that every memory of the protagonist's childhood centers on sex – also raises questions about her reliability as a narrator. The various men of the novel blur into a depersonalized collage of grabbing hands, jeering voices, and erect penises, anonymous, interchangeable ciphers in the text's endlessly superimposed scenarios of violence and violation.

A therapeutic language of trauma and sexual abuse lies ready to hand, yet Jones's novel anticipates and forestalls such interpretation, even as it undercuts any attempt to find a motive for the protagonist's actions. She is assailed on all sides by officers, lawyers, and therapists urging her to confess, prompting her to bare her feelings, invoking explanations of domestic abuse, sexual jealousy, a crime of passion, madness. Yet she refuses to open up, to explain or rationalize her actions; instead, she covers up her traces and changes her story, as she confuses events, blurs memories with dreams, utters evasive or enigmatic sentences. What she authors is a non-testimony, in which the facts surrounding the murder of her lover are never cleared up, as well as a non-confession, a refusal to surrender any scrap of interiority. Her outburst "Don't you explain me, don't you explain me, don't you explain me" is a patent injunction to the reader, underscored by premonitory examples of bad, negligent, or overly intrusive listeners in the novel.[23] And yet critics, it seems, cannot resist the lure of causal explanation, diagnosing the protagonist's silence as either pathological or empowering, subversive or passive. It is in fact *im*passive: a blank, unyielding surface that repels interpretation and cancels out an entire repertoire of hermeneutical possibilities, that calls on us to judge and yet mercilessly undercuts all our criteria of judgment.

As with Baudelaire, violence *in* the text bleeds into the violence *of* the text: the wielding of words as weapons to intensify and amplify its aesthetics of shock. Jones's novel is composed of jarring juxtapositions, crude or sexually explicit phrases, violations of norms and sensibilities, as the protagonist persists in breaching protocols of decency and decorum, bluntly naming what is usually unacknowledged: menstrual blood, belches and farts, the smell of genitalia. Sexual desire is ruthlessly de-idealized, recentered in a body that leaks and smells, that devours and defecates, though there is nothing remotely Rabelaisian about this bleak portrayal of physical frailty. Indeed, such transgressions seem motivated less by a desire to defy social or ethical norms than an uncanny indifference to them. After poisoning her lover, Eva describes how she leaves his hotel room and goes to a bar.

> I ate, drank beer. I ate plenty. I was already full from the cabbage and sausage he'd fed me, but it was good to eat again, to think about being naked and being taken. No, fucked. To think of my legs wide open, and my fingers up his ass.[24]

This flat Camus-like delivery relentlessly underscores a striking lack of guilt, anxiety, or other morally inflected emotions, while highlighting the incongruity of sexual appetite in the midst of catastrophe. Eva's words repel any potential surges of empathy or identification; there is a blankness about them that blocks the reader's effort to impose a standard repertoire of psychological, political, or moral frameworks. Like her interlocutors, we cannot help but feel that she is "too serene," her disassociation unnerving in its very inscrutability, its refusal to offer familiar footholds for interpretation. The protagonist's lack of shock summons forth the reader's own, as Jones's novel stages an attack, not just on our ethical sensibilities, but on the procedures by which we impute meaning to works of fiction.

Claudia Tate has lamented what she sees as a programmatic response to African-American fiction that draws all its energies from clearly limned categories of racial oppression and struggles for social justice. Such a subordination of the psychic to the social, she proposes, fails to do justice to aspects of black texts that do not lend themselves to such political recuperation: representations of confused and contradictory desires, enigmatic swirls of emotion, anti-social or self-destructive longings. Jones's novel, in this light, reveals a remarkable willingness to engage those recalcitrant and illegible aspects of the self that remain outside the purview of a redemptive racial politics, to embrace an aesthetic that is quintessentially tragic rather than romantic.[25] And yet, its ambivalent critical reception, grounded in concerns that it panders to racist prejudice, underscores the variable histories pressing down on an aesthetic of shock. While Baudelaire's or Camus's espousal of the pathological is commonly hailed as a heroic assault on bourgeois morality, such license is less freely granted to writers with more tenuous claims to aesthetic authority. Graphic portrayals of erotic violence in the tradition of European modernism often accrue a philosophical or even spiritual luster, but such portrayals are likely to resonate differently when dramatized through black bodies already burdened with presumptions of hypersexuality and aggression. *Eva's Man*, which occupies an uneasy place in the African-American literary canon while remaining outside the purview of advocates of transgression and self-shattering, underscores that an aesthetic of shock, whatever the power of its assault on our conventional categories of thought, remains soaked in sociocultural meanings.

We are all too accustomed to hearing critics extolling the insurgent energies of their favorite artwork or, alternately, lamenting the neutralization and cooption of shock by the forces of late capitalist modernity. In both its utopian and elegiac versions, shock is frequently burdened with meanings it cannot sustain, thanks to what I have called an ethos of avant-gardism, a chain of programmatic beliefs about the necessary relations between aesthetic novelty, perceptual jolts, and impending social upheaval. Such an ethos, it should be said, bears little relationship to individual works of the historical avant-garde, which continue to intrigue us precisely because of their ability to exceed the bounds of any such programmatic temporality.[26]

129

Yet the tenuousness of such chains of equivalence does not negate the phenomenological actuality of shock; audiences of various stripes still testify to feeling disturbed, disoriented, or disgusted by specific works of art. That shock fails to unleash a social cataclysm does not render it less salient as an element of aesthetic response. The discourse of the sublime, for example, bears eloquent witness to the experiential impact of art, its power to wreak havoc on our conceptual frames and commonsense assumptions, even though it pays scant heed to the ways in which such assaults are all too quickly re-mythologized within the discourse of the art world.[27] What we find shocking, moreover, is not merely a matter of formal innovation, stylistic subversion, or unconventionality for its own sake; it is also tied to contents of consciousness that have not yet been processed. An aesthetic of shock hooks up to all that we find grisly or abhorrent, to warring impulses of desire and disgust, subterranean dramas of psychic anxiety and ambivalence. It is far from evident, in this respect, that we are more emancipated than our ancestors, or that we could ever extricate ourselves from the dense weave of taboos and prohibitions that make up the fabric of human cultures. As long as we find ourselves prone to evasion, euphemism, and denial, as long as we flinch away from reminders of our material and mortal existence as fragile composites of blood, bone, and tissue, shock will continue to find a place in art.

Yet its effects must also be characterized as uncertain, unstable, and difficult to calibrate: shaking up consciousness is a strenuous and far from straightforward enterprise. If shock aims too low, its efforts to provoke are likely to go entirely unremarked or to risk being mocked as lame, tame, or risible. At any given moment, audiences are likely to have become immune or indifferent to the impact of certain subjects or styles of representation, to remain irritatingly unperturbed by what aims to disturb. Conversely, if shock-effects are ratcheted up too high, they are likely to trigger intense waves of revulsion or indignation that drive audiences out of theaters or cause them to slam shut their books, cutting off all further engagement with the work of art. When shock becomes too shocking, in other words, it cancels itself out in kamikaze fashion by prematurely terminating its own effects. Shock thus teeters precariously between the threat of two forms of failure, caught between the potential humiliation of audience indifference and the permanent risk of outright and outraged refusal. An aesthetic that assaults our psyches and assails our vulnerabilities turns out to be all too vulnerable to the vagaries of audience response.

# Conclusion

Disentangling individual strands of reader response and sticking them under the microscope one at a time for a closer look is, to be sure, a highly artificial exercise. Our reactions to works of art are never so decisively parceled out, so neatly swept into separate and self-contained piles. I plead guilty to imposing a tentative taxonomy onto forms of engagement that are more truthfully described as messy, blurred, compounded, and contradictory. Such an approach also seems at odds with my desire to capture something of the grain and texture of everyday aesthetic experience. If the act of reading fuses cognitive and affective impulses, if it looks outward to the world as well as inward to the self, then isolating and scrutinizing these intermeshed components looks suspiciously like an exercise in academic hairsplitting.

What justifies such an approach, I hope, is that it allows for individualized, fine-tuned descriptions of aspects of reading that have suffered the repeated ignominy of cursory or cavalier treatment. Thanks to the institutional entrenchment of negative aesthetics, a spectrum of reader responses has been ruled out of court in literary theory, deemed shamefully naïve at best, and rationalist, reactionary, or total-izing at worst. Shifting the grounds of debate requires a single-minded clarification of the caliber and qualities of such responses, as they play themselves out in the relations between individual acts of read-ing and a broader social field. The payoff for proceeding this way, in other words, is the hope of getting a better handle on how and why we read that steers clear of finalized formulae and preemptive or programmatic conclusions, that looks anew at what we have assured ourselves we already know. What literary studies sorely needs at this point is not just a micro-politics but a micro-aesthetics.

In practice, of course, the modes of engagement I outline remain intimately and sometimes indissolubly intertwined. Any social knowledge we gain from reading, for example, requires that a text solicit and capture our attention. Mimesis is mediated by multiple devices designed to lure in readers and to keep them hooked: suspense-filled plots, fine-tuned verbal mimicry, elaborate descriptions of imaginary drawing-rooms, renditions of who-said-what-to-whom that replicate the intimacy and intrigue of gossip. The enlargement of the reader's understanding is steered not only by formal devices and literary techniques, but also by the magical illusions, imaginative associations and emotional susceptibilities that such techniques call into being. Any attempt to develop a purely cognitive account of the value of reading runs the risk of overlooking the co-dependence of mimesis and magic, of enlightenment and enchantment.

The everyday phrase "the shock of recognition" draws together the titles of my other two chapters, underscoring that glimpsing aspects of oneself in a literary text is a far from straightforward experience. The seemingly rationalist idea of recognition turns out to rely on an interplay of sameness and difference, familiarity and strangeness; what the mirror shows us is not always what we hoped or expected to see. While recognition is an indispensable moment in interpretation, it is actualized in disparate aesthetic, personal, and sociopolitical registers. Conversely, a cognitive and interpretive component clings even to our most visceral reactions, as our minds and bodies register the unnerving impact of the disgusting, violent, or obscene. The self is never entirely or irrevocably shattered by art's assault on convention or flaunting of taboos; the experience of aesthetic shock, however hair-raising or gut-wrenching it turns out to be, does not dissolve the meshes of symbolization and social meaning.

Finally, any hard-and-fast opposition between shock and enchantment implied by my argument can be effortlessly deconstructed. Enchantment attracts such intense animus because it is perceived to rob readers of their autonomy and will power, turning them into little more than automatons or sleepwalkers. The pleasure of enchantment turns out to be thoroughly *unheimlich* at its core, underscoring the limits of our attempts at self-possession and signaling the sheer opacity and intractability of subjectivity. Conversely, even as shock summons forth negative reactions such as disgust, repulsion, or horror, the willingness of many readers and viewers to undergo such emotions, indeed, to actively seek them out, testifies to its paradoxical allure. Contemporary audiences reap a variety of pleasures from such visceral responses, whether the bracing knowledge of facing one's worst fears by staring into the abyss, the masochistic bliss of being pummeled and punched by a work of art, or the satisfaction of belonging to a subcultural coterie in advance of more conventional taste.

While these elements of aesthetic experience exist in states of interdependence and symbiosis, I want to resist conflating them or minimizing their differences by treating them as essentially minor or peripheral variations on a common theme. One advantage of splicing up the spectrum of literary response is that it underscores not only the different ways that different people read but also the different ways in which the same individuals read, the dramatic fluctuations in modes and motives of aesthetic engagement. While working my way through recent publications intent on resuscitating such concepts as literary truth and aesthetic pleasure, I have been struck by the cursory manner in which such terms are often handled. Either their meaning is gestured toward in only the vaguest, most token of terms, in a return to a pre-theory era of clubby consensus, or else they are characterized in quite insular and often genre-specific ways. Not only do critics continue to fixate on such academic sacred cows as "difficulty" (even pleasure invariably turns out to be "difficult pleasure"), but they advance general theses about the purpose and value of literature that turn out to be rooted in the specific features of lyric poetry, or the realist novel, or avant-garde prose. Even as universalisms are widely and piously abjured in contemporary scholarship, many critics still do violence to the myriad forms of reading by cramming them into a single analytical or theoretical box.

Four boxes constitute, no doubt, only a modest improvement, but they signal a structural advance in forcing us to come to grips with the variety of aesthetic experiences and multiple axes of literary value. To acknowledge multiple criteria of value is not to imply that anything goes, to advocate a relativist standpoint, or to suggest that we can never be critical of the aesthetic judgments of others. It is simply to recognize that works of art can be appreciated for a host of good reasons. Looking back at the examples of readers and reading that have cropped up in the preceding pages, I would be hard-pressed to identify any one feature they all have in common. Does anything really unite the women of late-nineteenth-century London seeing themselves in Hedda Gabler, the queer theorist enraptured by the thrilling impersonality of Austenite style, the contemporary reader harrowed yet intrigued by Gayl Jones's deadpan descriptions of violence, my own interest in Pablo Neruda's invocation of the sturdiness of everyday objects? Even such a modest handful of examples enfolds a multiplicity of motives, affects, interpretive strategies, and scenes of reading that are poorly served by catch-all appeals to aesthetic pleasure or the literariness of literature. To paraphrase Wittgenstein, there is no single fiber that runs through the entire thread of reader response.

Literary theory is still struggling to come to terms with such plurality; it has manifest difficulty in recognizing that literature may be valued for different, even incommensurable reasons. Instead, it remains enamored of the absolute, dazzled by the grand gesture, seeking the key to all the mythologies in the idea of alterity or sublimity, desire or defamiliarization, ethical enrichment or political transgression. Must we really distinguish so categorically between the damned and the saved, banishing to the outer darkness all the riff-raff or renegades oblivious to our own preferred hermeneutic or the dazzling apercus of our favored theorist? I remain unpersuaded that such gestures of excommunication advance either the aesthetics or the politics of literary interpretation. In this respect, as in a number of others, this book can only be called a defective or delinquent manifesto.

# Notes

## Introduction

1  Harold Bloom, *How to Read and Why* (New York: Scribner's, 2001), p. 22.
2  Michael Warner observes that "critical reading is the folk ideology of a learned profession, so close to us that we seldom feel the need to explain it." See his "Uncritical Reading," in Jane Gallop, ed., *Polemic: Critical or Uncritical* (New York: Routledge, 2004), p. 14.
3  Eve Kosofsky Sedgwick, "Paranoid Reading and Reparative Reading: or, You're so Paranoid, You Probably Think This Introduction is About You," in Eve Kosofsky Sedgwick, ed., *Novel Gazing: Queer Readings in Fiction* (Durham, NC: Duke University Press, 1997). Sedgwick's critique of the hermeneutics of suspicion has been especially influential; there are, of course, many other critiques, from varying perspectives. See, for example, Charles Altieri, *Canons and Consequences: Reflections on the Ethical Force of Imaginative Ideals* (Evanston, IL: Northwestern University Press, 1990); Eugene Goodheart, *The Skeptical Disposition in Contemporary Criticism* (Princeton, NJ: Princeton University Press, 1991); Umberto Eco, *Interpretation and Overinterpretation* (Cambridge: Cambridge University Press, 1992); Mark Edmundson, *Why Read?* (New York: Bloomsbury, 2004).
4  Sedgwick, "Paranoid Reading and Reparative Reading," p. 35.
5  Marjorie Perloff, "Crisis in the Humanities? Reconfiguring Literary Study for the Twenty-first Century," in her *Differentials: Poetry, Poetics, Pedagogy* (Tuscaloosa: University of Alabama Press, 2004), p. 7.
6  Thomas Docherty, *Aesthetic Democracy* (Stanford, CA: Stanford University Press, 2006).
7  Lennard J. Davis, *Resisting Novels: Ideology and Fiction* (New York: Methuen, 1987), pp. 224–225.
8  Ellen Rooney, "Form and Contentment," *MLQ*, 61, 1 (2000), p. 38.

9  William James, *Pragmatism* (Cambridge, MA: Harvard University Press, 1975), pp. 17–18.

10  Amanda Anderson, *The Way We Argue Now: A Study in the Cultures of Theory* (Princeton, NJ: Princeton University Press, 2006).

11  Ato Quayson, *Calibrations: Reading for the Social* (Minneapolis: University of Minnesota Press, 2003), p. xxi.

12  See, among many others, Nancy Armstrong, *Desire and Domestic Fiction: A Political History of the Novel* (Oxford: Oxford University Press, 1987); Rita Felski, *The Gender of Modernity* (Cambridge, MA: Harvard University Press, 1995); Susan Stanford Friedman, *Mappings: Feminism and the Cultural Geographies of Encounter* (Princeton, NJ: Princeton University Press, 1998); Sharon Marcus, *Between Women: Friendship, Desire and Marriage in Victorian England* (Princeton, NJ: Princeton University Press, 2007); Mary Poovey, *Uneven Developments: The Political Work of Gender in Mid-Victorian England* (Chicago: University of Chicago Press, 1988); Jane Tompkins, *Sensational Designs: The Cultural Work of American Fiction 1790–1860* (Oxford: Oxford University Press, 1985).

13  Wai Chee Dimock, "A Theory of Resonance," *PMLA*, 112, 5 (1997), p. 1061.

14  On this point, see Anderson, *The Way We Argue Now*, and Frank Farrell, *Why Does Literature Matter?* (Ithaca, NY: Cornell University Press, 2004).

15  John Guillory, "The Ethics of Reading," in Marjorie Garber et al., eds., *The Turn to Ethics* (New York: Routledge, 2000).

16  David Carter and Kay Ferres, "The Public Life of Literature," in Tony Bennett and David Carter, eds., *Culture in Australia: Policies, Publics and Programs* (Cambridge: Cambridge University Press, 2001). These issues are also rehearsed in Dave Beech and John Roberts, eds., *The Philistine Controversy* (London: Verso, 2002).

17  We could add to this list the intriguing new work on doxa. See Ruth Amossy, "Introduction to the Study of Doxa," *Poetics Today*, 23, 3 (2002), pp. 369–394. I have also been inspired by Antoine Compagnon's *Literature, Theory and Common Sense* (Princeton, NJ: Princeton University Press, 2004) and by Toril Moi's *What is a Woman? And Other Essays* (Oxford: Oxford University Press, 1999).

18  Richard Shusterman, *Surface and Depth: Dialectics of Criticism and Culture* (Ithaca, NY: Cornell University Press, 2002).

19  Noel Carroll, "Beauty and the Genealogy of Art Theory," in his *Beyond Aesthetics: Philosophical Essays* (Cambridge: Cambridge University Press, 2001).

20  Steven Connor, "CP: Or a Few Don'ts by a Cultural Phenomenologist," *Parallax*, 5, 2 (1991), p. 18.

21  See, for example, Heather Love, *Feeling Backward: Loss and the Politics of Queer History* (Cambridge, MA: Harvard University Press, 2007); Sarah Ahmed, *Queer Phenomenology* (Durham, NC: Duke University Press, 2006).

22  In contrast to much recent ethical criticism, however, I do not see ethics as purely a matter of particularity and otherness. In our engagement with others, we surely seek not only a recognition of our differences but also an openness to potential commonalities and affinities. See Adam Zachary Newton, *Narrative Ethics* (Cambridge, MA: Harvard University Press, 1995); Robert Eaglestone, *Ethical Criticism* (Edinburgh: Edinburgh University Press, 1998).

23  I borrow this term from J. M. Bernstein, *Against Voluptuous Bodies: Late Modernism and the Meaning of Painting* (Stanford, CA: Stanford University Press, 2006). Bernstein uses it, however, in the context of an Adorno-esque argument about the role of art in a rationalized and reified society; I am not at all confident that he would endorse such an ecumenical use of his phrase.

24  John Frow, *Cultural Studies and Cultural Value* (Oxford: Oxford University Press, 1995), p. 134. See also Barbara Herrnstein Smith, "Value/Evaluation," in Frank Lentricchia and Thomas McLaughlin, eds., *Critical Terms for Literary Study* (Chicago: University of Chicago Press, 1995); Steven Connor, *Theory and Cultural Value* (Oxford: Blackwell, 1992); Simon Frith, *Performing Rites: On the Value of Popular Music* (Cambridge, MA: Harvard University Press, 1998).

## Chapter 1   Recognition

1  Oscar Wilde, *The Picture of Dorian Gray* (Harmondsworth: Penguin, 1985), p. 158.

2  Pankaj Mishra, *The Romantics* (New York: Vintage, 2000), p. 155.

3  Hans-Georg Gadamer, *Truth and Method* (New York: Continuum, 2003), p. 114.

4  Richard Barney, *Plots of Enlightenment: Education and the Novel in Eighteenth-Century England* (Stanford, CA: Stanford University Press, 1999).

5  Marcel Proust, *Remembrance of Things Past* (New York: Random House, 1981), 3, p. 949.

6  Charles Taylor, "The Politics of Recognition," in Charles Taylor et al., *Multiculturalism: Examining the Politics of Recognition* (Princeton, NJ: Princeton University Press, 1994), p. 26. For the Fraser/Honneth debate, see Nancy Fraser and Axel Honneth, *Redistribution or Recognition? A Political-Philosophical Exchange* (London: Verso, 2001).

7  Ludwig Wittgenstein, *Philosophical Investigations* (Oxford: Blackwell, 2001), p. 154.

8  Majid Yar, "Recognition and the Politics of Human(e) Desire," in Scott Lash and Mike Featherstone, eds., *Recognition and Difference* (London: Sage, 2002).

9   Chantal Mouffe, *The Democratic Paradox* (London: Verso, 2000); Judith Butler, "Longing for Recognition," in her *Undoing Gender* (New York: Routledge, 2004).

10   Daniel Stern, *The Interpersonal World of the Infant: A View from Psychoanalysis and Developmental Psychology* (New York: Basic Books, 1985), p. 162.

11   G. H. Mead, *Mind, Self and Society* (Chicago: University of Chicago Press, 1962), p. 164.

12   Suzanne Juhasz, *Reading from the Heart: Women, Literature and the Search for True Love* (Harmondsworth: Penguin, 1994), p. 5.

13   Elizabeth Robins, *Ibsen and the Actress* (London: Hogarth Press, 1928), p. 18.

14   Murray Smith, *Engaging Characters: Fiction, Emotion, and the Cinema* (Oxford: Clarendon Press, 1995).

15   See, for example, Don Kuiken, David S. Miall, and Shelley Sikora, "Forms of Self-Implication in Literary Reading," *Poetics Today*, 25, 2 (2004), pp. 171–203.

16   Quoted in Susan Torrey Barstow, "'Hedda is All of Us': Late-Victorian Women at the Matinee," *Victorian Studies* 43, 3 (2001), p. 405.

17   Lou Andreas-Salomé, *Ibsen's Women* (Reading Ridge, CT: Black Swan, 1985), p. 130.

18   Sarah Ahmed, *Strange Encounters: Embodied Others in Post-Coloniality* (London: Routledge, 2000), p. 3.

19   See Maria Pia Lara, *Moral Textures: Feminist Narratives in the Public Sphere* (Berkeley: University of California Press, 1999).

20   Mishra, *The Romantics*, p. 118.

21   Mishra, *The Romantics*, p. 250.

22   Mishra, *The Romantics*, p. 250.

23   Shu-mei Shih, "Global Literature and the Technologies of Recognition," *PMLA*, 119, 1 (2004), pp. 16–30.

24   Terence Cave, *Recognition* (Oxford: Oxford University Press, 1988), p. 233.

25   Stephen White, *Sustaining Affirmation: The Strengths of Weak Ontology in Political Theory* (Princeton, NJ: Princeton University Press, 2000), p. 5.

26   Terry Castle, "Afterword," in Laura Doan and Jay Prosser, eds., *Palatable Poison: Critical Perspectives on "The Well of Loneliness"* (New York: Columbia University Press, 2003), p. 400.

27   Heather Love, *Feeling Backwards: Loss and the Politics of Queer History* (Cambridge, MA: Harvard University Press, 2007), p. 100.

28   Alexander García Düttman, *Between Cultures: Tensions in the Struggle for Recognition* (London: Verso, 2000).

29   R. Radhakrishnan, "The Use and Abuse of Multiculturalism," in his *Theory in an Uneven World* (Oxford: Blackwell, 2003).

30   Steven C. Rockefeller, "Comment," in Taylor et al., *Multiculturalism*, p. 97; Juhasz, *Reading from the Heart*.

31  Patchen Markell, *Bound By Recognition* (Princeton, NJ: Princeton University Press, 2003), p. 3.

32  Michel Foucault, "Nietzsche, Genealogy, History," in his *Language, Counter-Memory, Practice* (Ithaca, NY: Cornell University Press, 1977), p. 153.

33  Christopher Prendergast, *The Order of Mimesis* (Cambridge: Cambridge University Press, 1986), p. 22. On the fallibility and inescapability of self-knowledge, see Richard Moran, *Authority and Estrangement: An Essay on Self-Knowledge* (Princeton, NJ: Princeton University Press, 2001).

## Chapter 2   Enchantment

1   Joseph Boone, *Libidinal Currents: Sexuality and the Shaping of Modernism* (Chicago: University of Chicago Press, 1998), p. 20.

2   Boone, *Libidinal Currents*, p. 1.

3   Gustave Flaubert, *Madame Bovary* (New York: W. W. Norton, 1965), p. 163.

4   Quoted in Suzi Gablik, *The Reenchantment of Art* (London: Thames and Hudson, 1991), p. 26.

5   Stephen Greenblatt, "Resonance and Wonder," in Ivan Karp and Steven D. Lavine, eds., *The Poetics and Politics of Museum Display* (Washington, DC: Smithsonian Institute Press, 1991), p. 49.

6   Bertolt Brecht, *A Short Organum for the Theatre*, in John Willett, ed., *Brecht on Theatre: The Development of an Aesthetic* (New York: Hill and Wang, 1964), p. 187.

7   Michael Fried, *Absorption and Theatricality: Painting and Beholder in the Age of Diderot* (Chicago: University of Chicago Press, 1980).

8   Max Weber, "Science as a Vocation," in H. H. Gerth and C. Wright Mills, eds., *From Max Weber: Essays in Sociology* (New York: Oxford University Press, 1968), p. 139.

9   Jane Bennett, *The Enchantment of Modern Life: Attachments, Crossings, and Ethics* (Princeton, NJ: Princeton University Press, 2001).

10  See, for example, Saurabh Dube, "Introduction: Enchantments of Modernity," special issue on "Enduring Enchantments," *South Atlantic Quarterly*, 101, 4 (2002), pp. 729–755; Birgit Meyer and Peter Pels, eds., *Magic and Modernity: Interfaces of Revelation and Concealment* (Stanford, CA: Stanford University Press, 2003).

11  Max Weber, "Objectivity in Social Science and Policy," in Edward A. Shils and Henry A. Finch, eds., *Max Weber on the Methodology of the Social Sciences*, (Glencoe, IL: Free Press, 1949), p. 10. For an amplification of this point, see Basit Bilal Koshul, *The Postmodern Significance of Max Weber's Legacy: Disenchanting Disenchantment* (New York: Palgrave, 2005).

12  J. Hillis Miller, *On Literature* (London: Routledge, 2002).

13 Jonathan Rose, *The Intellectual Life of the British Working Classes* (New Haven, CT: Yale University Press, 2001), p. 127.

14 Janice Radway, *A Feeling for Books: The Book-of-the-Month Club, Literary Taste, and Middle-Class Desire* (Chapel Hill: University of North Carolina Press, 1997), p. 13; Lynne Pearce, *Feminism and the Politics of Reading* (London: Arnold, 1997).

15 Marie-Laure Ryan, *Narrative as Virtual Reality: Immersion and Interactivity in Literature and Electronic Media* (Baltimore: Johns Hopkins University Press, 2001), p. 98.

16 Eve Kosofsky Sedgwick, "Queer and Now," *Tendencies* (Durham, NC: Duke University Press, 1993), p. 3.

17 D. A. Miller, *Jane Austen, or the Secret of Style* (Princeton, NJ: Princeton University Press, 2003), p. 8.

18 Elaine Scarry, *On Beauty and Being Just* (Princeton, NJ: Princeton University Press, 1999); Denis Donoghue, *Speaking of Beauty* (New Haven, CT: Yale University Press, 2004).

19 Fredric Jameson, *A Singular Modernity: Essay on the Ontology of the Present* (London: Verso, 2002), pp. 177–179.

20 John Carey, *What Good are the Arts?* (London: Faber and Faber, 2005), p. 23.

21 Manuel Puig, *Kiss of the Spider Woman* (New York: Vintage, 1991), pp. 54–55.

22 Edgar Morin, *The Cinema, or The Imaginary Man* (Minneapolis: University of Minnesota Press, 2005), p. 16.

23 Bill Brown, *A Sense of Things: The Object Matter of American Literature* (Chicago: University of Chicago Press, 2003).

24 Greenblatt, "Resonance and Wonder." For a critique of this distinction, see Wai Chee Dimock, "A Theory of Resonance," *PMLA*, 112, 5 (1997), pp. 1046–1059.

25 Michel Poizat, *The Angel's Cry: Beyond the Pleasure Principle in Opera* (Ithaca, NY: Cornell University Press, 1992); Wayne Koestenbaum, *The Queen's Throat: Opera, Homosexuality, and the Mystery of Desire* (New York: Da Capo, 1993).

26 Theodor Adorno and Max Horkheimer, *The Dialectic of Enlightenment* (Stanford, CA: Stanford University Press, 2002), p. 26. See also Linda Phyllis Austern's helpful essay, "'Teach Me to Hear Mermaids Singing: Embodiments of (Acoustic) Pleasure and Danger in the Modern West," in Linda Phyllis Austern and Inna Naroditskaya, eds., *Music of the Sirens* (Bloomington: Indiana University Press, 2006).

27 On voice and possession, see Susan Stewart, *Poetry and the Fate of the Senses* (Chicago: University of Chicago Press, 2002).

28 Roland Barthes, *The Pleasure of the Text* (New York: Hill and Wang, 1976), p. 66.

29 Seamus Heaney, "Influences," *Boston Review* 14, 5 (1989).

30 Charles Bernstein, "Artifice of Absorption," in *A Poetics* (Cambridge, MA: Harvard University Press, 1992), pp. 52–53.

31  Bernstein, "Artifice of Absorption," p. 23.
32  Morin, *The Cinema*, p. 225.
33  Michael Saler, "'Clap if You Believe in Sherlock Holmes': Mass Culture and the Re-Enchantment of Modernity, c. 1890–c. 1940," *Historical Journal*, 46, 3 (2003), pp. 599–622, and "Modernity and Enchantment: A Historiographic Review," *American Historical Review*, 111, 3 (2006), pp. 692–716. See also Simon During, *Modern Enchantments: The Cultural Power of Secular Magic* (Cambridge, MA: Harvard University Press, 2002).
34  Barry Fuller, "Pleasure and Self-Loss in Reading," *ADE Bulletin*, 99 (Fall 1991).
35  I take the term "pre-evaluation" from Barbara Herrnstein Smith, "Value/Evaluation," in Frank Lentricchia and Thomas McLaughlin, eds., *Critical Terms for Literary Study* (Chicago: University of Chicago Press, 1995). A US newspaper recently persuaded a world-famous violinist to play incognito in a subway station and reported on the results. "Pearls Before Breakfast," *Washington Post*, April 8, 2007.

## Chapter 3    Knowledge

1  Morris Dickstein, *A Mirror in the Roadway: Literature and the Real World* (Princeton, NJ: Princeton University Press, 2005), p. 8.
2  Charles Taylor, *Sources of the Self: The Making of the Modern Identity* (Cambridge, MA: Harvard University Press, 1989).
3  Pierre Macherey, *A Theory of Literary Production* (London: Routledge, 1978), p. 133.
4  Paul de Man, *Blindness and Insight* (Minneapolis: University of Minnesota Press, 1983), p. 17.
5  Gerald Graff, *Literature Against Itself: Literary Ideas in Modern Society* (Chicago: Ivan Dee, 1995), pp. 20–21.
6  Philip Weinstein, *Unknowing: The Work of Modernist Fiction* (Ithaca, NY: Cornell University Press, 2005).
7  Christopher Prendergast, *The Order of Mimesis: Balzac, Stendhal, Nerval, Flaubert* (Cambridge: Cambridge University Press, 1986); Antoine Compagnon, *Literature, Theory, and Common Sense* (Princeton, NJ: Princeton University Press, 2004).
8  Marjorie Perloff, *Differentials: Poetry, Poetics, Pedagogy* (Tuscaloosa: University of Alabama Press, 2004), p. 17.
9  John Frow, *Genre* (London: Routledge, 2006), p. 12.
10  Paul Ricoeur, "Time and Narrative: Threefold *Mimesis*," in his *Time and Narrative*, vol. 1 (Chicago: University of Chicago Press, 1984).
11  Ricoeur, *Time and Narrative*, pp. 72–74. See also Rita Felski, "Plots," in her *Literature After Feminism* (Chicago: University of Chicago Press, 2003).

12  Kenneth Dauber and Water Jost, "Introduction: The Varieties of Ordinary Language Criticism," in *Ordinary Language Criticism: Literary Thinking After Cavell After Wittgenstein* (Evanston, IL: Northwestern University Press, 2003), p. xx.

13  Prendergast, *The Order of Mimesis*, p. 21.

14  Edith Wharton, "Introduction to the 1936 Edition of The House of Mirth," in Carol J. Singley, ed., *Edith Wharton's The House of Mirth: A Casebook* (New York: Oxford University Press, 2003), p. 33.

15  Charles Altieri, *Act and Quality: A Theory of Literary Meaning and Humanistic Understanding* (Amherst: University of Massachusetts Press, 1981), p. 271.

16  Hayden White, *Tropics of Discourse: Essays in Cultural Criticism* (Baltimore: Johns Hopkins University Press, 1985), pp. 121–122.

17  Dorrit Cohn, *The Distinction of Fiction* (Baltimore: Johns Hopkins University Press, 1999).

18  Edith Wharton, *The House of Mirth*, ed. Martha Banta (Oxford: Oxford University Press, 1994), p. 7.

19  George Butte, *I Know that You Know that I Know: Narrating Subjects from Moll Flanders to Marnie* (Columbus: Ohio State University Press, 2004).

20  See, for example, Carol de Dobay Rifelj, *Reading the Other: Novels and the Problem of Other Minds* (Ann Arbor: University of Michigan Press, 1992); Martha Nussbaum, "The Window: Knowledge of Other Minds in Virginia Woolf's To the Lighthouse," *New Literary History*, 26, 4 (1995), pp. 731–753.

21  Alfred Schutz, *The Phenomenology of the Social World*, trans. George Walsh and Frederick Lehnhert (Chicago: Northwestern University Press, 1967).

22  Alex Woloch, *The One vs. The Many: Minor Characters and the Space of the Protagonist in the Novel* (Princeton, NJ: Princeton University Press, 2003).

23  Ken Hirschkop, *Mikhail Bakhtin: An Aesthetic for Democracy* (Oxford: Oxford University Press, 1999).

24  Evelyn Nien-Ming Chi'en, *Weird English* (Cambridge, MA: Harvard University Press, 2005).

25  Doris Sommer, *Proceed with Caution, when Engaged by Minority Writing in the Americas* (Cambridge, MA: Harvard University Press, 1999).

26  Richard Rossiter, "In His Own Words: The Life and Times of Tim Winton," in Richard Rossiter and Lyn Jacobs, eds., *Reading Tim Winton* (Sydney: Angus and Robertson, 1993), p. 11.

27  Tim Winton, *Cloudstreet* (New York: Simon and Schuster, 1991).

28  Peter Brooks, *Realist Vision* (New Haven, CT: Yale University Press, 2005), p. 210.

29  Elaine Freedgood, *The Ideas in Things: Fugitive Meaning in the Victorian Novel* (Chicago: University of Chicago Press, 2006).

30  Pablo Neruda, *Odes to Common Things*, trans. Ken Krabbenhoft (New York: Bulfinch, 1994), pp. 11–17.

31  Sara Ahmed, *Queer Phenomenology: Orientations, Objects, Others* (Durham, NC: Duke University Press, 2006), p. 164.
32  Neruda, *Odes to Common Things*, pp. 89–95.
33  Douglas Mao, *Solid Objects: Modernism and the Test of Production* (Princeton, NJ: Princeton University Press, 1998). See also Peter Schwenger, *The Tears of Things: Melancholy and Physical Objects* (Minneapolis: University of Minnesota Press, 2006).
34  Simon Critchley, *Things Merely Are* (London: Routledge, 2005); Rosemary Lloyd, *Shimmering in a Transformed Light: Writing the Still Life* (Ithaca, NY: Cornell University Press, 2005).
35  See Nelson Goodman, *Ways of Worldmaking* (Indianapolis: Hackett, 1978), p. 102.
36  Terry Eagleton, *Criticism and Ideology* (London: Verso, 1976).

## Chapter 4   Shock

1  Gianni Vattimo, *The Transparent Society* (Baltimore: Johns Hopkins University Press, 1992), pp. 47–51.
2  Lionel Trilling, "On the Teaching of Modern Literature," in his *Beyond Culture: Essays on Literature and Learning* (New York: Viking, 1965).
3  Fredric Jameson, "Postmodernism and Consumer Society," in Hal Foster, ed., *Postmodern Culture* (London: Pluto Press, 1983), p. 124.
4  Tristan Tzara, "Dada Manifesto 1918," in *Seven Dada Manifestos and Lampisteries*, trans. Barbara Wright (London: John Calder, 1977), p. 8.
5  Jean-Joseph Goux, "The Eclipse of Art," *Thesis Eleven*, 44 (1996), pp. 57–68.
6  Euripides, *The Bacchae*, in *Euripides V: The Complete Greek Tragedies* ed. David Grene and Richmond Lattimore (Chicago: University of Chicago Press, 1959), p. 204.
7  Jean-Pierre Vernant and Pierre Vidal Naquet, *Myth and Tragedy in Ancient Greece* (New York: Zone, 1990), p. 246.
8  Karl Heinz Bohrer, *Suddenness: On the Moment of Aesthetic Appearance* (New York: Columbia, 1994).
9  Wai Chee Dimock, "A Theory of Resonance," *PMLA*, 112, 5 (1997), pp. 1046–1059.
10  Heinrich von Kleist, *Penthesilea*, trans. Joel Agee (New York: Harper Collins, 1998), p. 128.
11  Kleist, *Penthesilea*, pp. 145–146.
12  Michel Chaouli, "Devouring Metaphor: Disgust and Taste in Kleist's *Penthesilea*," *German Quarterly*, 69, 2 (1996), p. 130.
13  Leo Bersani, *The Freudian Body: Psychoanalysis and Art* (New York: Columbia University Press, 1986), p. 70.
14  Jean Laplanche, "Notes on Afterwardness," in his *Essays on Otherness* (London: Routledge, 1999).

15  Walter Benjamin, "N [Re The Theory of Knowledge, Theory of Progress]," in Gary Smith, ed., *Benjamin – Philosophy, Aesthetics, History* (Chicago: University of Chicago Press, 1989), p. 50.

16  Elisabeth Ladenson, *Dirt for Art's Sake: Books on Trial from Madame Bovary to Lolita* (Ithaca, NY: Cornell University Press, 2007), p. xvi.

17  Walter Benjamin, "Some Motifs in Baudelaire," in *Charles Baudelaire: A Lyric Poet in the Era of High Capitalism* (London: Verso, 1983), p. 116. See also Vaheed. K. Ramazani, "Writing in Pain: Baudelaire, Benjamin, Haussmann," *Boundary 2*, 23, 2 (1996), pp. 199–224.

18  Charles Baudelaire, "La Charogne/A Carcass," in Marthiel and Jackson Mathews, eds., *The Flowers of Evil* (New York: New Directions, 1955).

19  Pierre Bourdieu, *Distinction: A Social Critique of the Judgment of Taste* (Cambridge, MA: Harvard University Press, 1984).

20  William Ian Miller, *The Anatomy of Disgust* (Cambridge, MA: Harvard University Press, 1997), p. 49.

21  Margaret Oliphant, "Sensation Novels," quoted in Deborah Wynne, *The Sensation Novel and the Victorian Family Magazine* (New York: Palgrave, 2001), p. 44.

22  Kathy Acker, *Blood and Guts in High School* (New York: Grove, 1994); Elfriede Jelinek, *The Piano Teacher* (London: Serpent's Tail, 1989); Helen Zahavi, *Dirty Weekend* (London: Flamingo, 1991); Sarah Kane, *Complete Plays* (London: Methuen, 2001).

23  Gayl Jones, *Eva's Man* (Boston: Beacon Press, 1976), p. 173.

24  Jones, *Eva's Man*, p. 130.

25  Claudia Tate, *Psychoanalysis and Black Novels: Desire and the Protocols of Race* (New York: Oxford University Press, 1998); David Scott, *Conscripts of Modernity: The Tragedy of Colonial Enlightenment* (Durham, NC: Duke University Press, 2004).

26  Hal Foster remarks that to take the romantic rhetoric of the avant-garde, with its language of rupture and revolution, at its word is to mistake crucial dimensions of its practice. See "Who's Afraid of the Neo-Avant-Garde?" in his *The Return of the Real: The Avant-Garde at the End of the Century* (Cambridge, MA: MIT Press, 1996).

27  Jean-François Lyotard, "The Sublime and the Avant-Garde," in his *The Inhuman: Reflections on Time* (Stanford, CA: Stanford University Press, 1992).

# Index

# Index

147

# Index

149

# Index

# Index

151

# Index